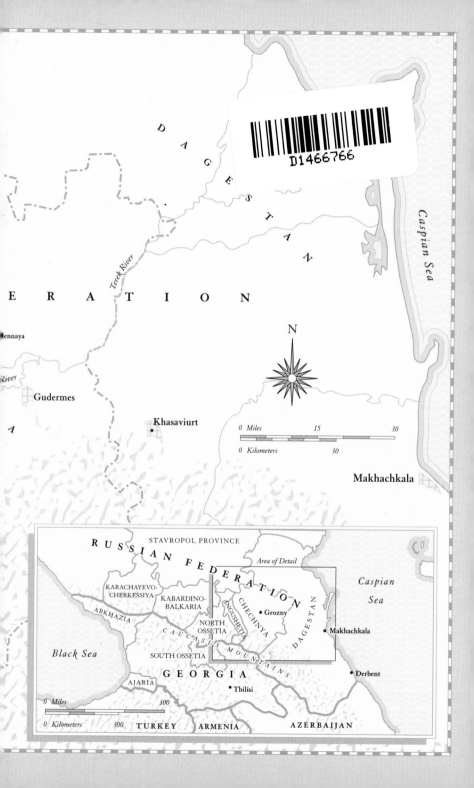

Chienne de Guerre

A Woman Reporter

Behind the Lines

of the War in Chechnya

Anne Nivat

Translated by Susan Darnton

PublicAffairs New York

Book design and composition by Mark McGarry, Texas Type & Book Works
Set in Adobe Garamond

The French edition of *Chienne de Guerre* was published by © Librarie Arthème
Fayard, 2000.

Library of Congress Cataloging-in-Publication Data
Nivat, Anne.
[Chienne de guerre. English]
Chienne de guerre / by Anne Nivat. —1st ed.
p. cm.
Translation from French; text is in English.
ISBN 1-58648-044-8
1. Chechnëï (Russia)—History—Civil War, 1994–
2. Nivat, Anne—Journeys—Russia (Federation)—Chechnëï. I. Title.
DK511.C37N5813   2001
947.5 2—DC21   00-054739

FIRST EDITION
1 3 5 7 9 10 8 6 4 2

To my Father

Acknowledgments

I would like to thank Bob Kaiser and Marvin Kalb who were not totally put off by my "horrible stories" from Chechnya, and who helped me find an American publisher; Andrew Paulson, who managed to keep in contact with me while I was in Chechnya; Fiona Hill, Sarah Mendelson, and Elin Suleymanov who understood what I was experiencing on the spot; Svetlana Alexeieff-Rockwell, Elena Levin, Frances Forte, Cheryl Hutchinson, and Lucille Wymer who didn't understand. It was better that way; they helped me recover. Lastly, thanks to Dan Williams and Lucia Annunciata. I had the immense and rare pleasure of writing these pages in their house on the island of Capri.

Preface

This book is an account of the war in Chechnya as I saw and lived it. At the time, I was working as a freelance reporter for two French dailies, *Libération* and *Ouest-France*. I had been living in Moscow for exactly a year. I was a young, inexperienced journalist, and I was having quite a hard time finding enough newspapers to print my stuff so that I could earn a living and establish my reputation. But I was thrilled to be realizing one of my earliest dreams: to be living and working in Moscow.

Russia had always been a shared passion in my family. My parents often invited Russian guests to our home for soirées. Writers, artists, professors, and dissidents of all kinds passed through our villa, which was located in an area of France close to the Swiss border. My father, a professor at the University of Geneva, brought the Russians home with him, slipping them discreetly past the passport inspectors at the border (there were inevitably visa problems). As a child, I was fascinated by these bearded, rather wild-eyed men, who smelled of foreign cigarettes. Dinner lasted for hours and the table talk was entirely in Russian. Though I couldn't understand a word of it, this language sounded strangely familiar to my young ears. I was curious by nature, and I was eager to know what the adults were discussing. It was my mother who finally taught me Russian. She was a teacher in the secondary school of our provincial town. Six of us studied Russian together for five years. We passed the baccalaureate as a group.

I left my comfortable life in Paris with a doctorate in political science—my focus was Russian affairs—in my pocket. I was twenty-five years old. Prague was my first destination. I spent the next three years in the Czech Republic, figuring out how to report "from the field." This was my first encounter with "Anglo-Saxon" journalism, as it's rather ironically known in France. I was working as a staff writer for *Transitions*, an English-language magazine published by George Soros and his Open Society Institute. Two people I met there played an influential role in my life: Michael Kaufman, who was enjoying a two years' leave of absence from the *New York Times* to serve as editor-in-chief of the magazine, and Josephine Schmidt, then managing editor of *Transitions*, now on the staff of the *New York Times*. These two mentors left me completely free to choose my own stories within the immense geographical area we covered, the ex-Communist countries of Europe and the former Soviet Union. They also edited the "travel accounts" I brought back from the field. My first trip to the Caucasus was as a reporter for *Transitions*. I traveled through Chechnya in 1996, at the end of the first Russian-Chechen war. I returned to the area at the end of January 1997 to witness the special presidential elections and the victory of Aslan Maskhadov, the current Chechen pro-independence president whose legitimacy Moscow still refuses to recognize.

The hospitality of the people of the Caucasus, their customs and mores, struck a chord in me. I felt, as I often do when I am at some distance from the West, strangely safe and in touch with myself. The mountainous landscape reminded me of the Alps of my childhood. Perhaps this explains why—after a year's break as a Fulbright Fellow at Harvard's Russian Research Center—I decided to return to southern Russia.

I was only sorry not to have returned sooner. For it is during the period between the two wars, from 1997 to 1999, where we must search for the seeds of the second Russian-Chechen conflict, a conflict that continues to this day. If we journalists ignore areas where nothing dramatic is happening—or where we imagine that nothing is happening—how can we pretend to analyze conflict when it arises? I do not claim to understand the origins of the Russian-Chechen confrontation. I can only sketch its contours and paint to the best of my abilities a faithful picture of what I saw and experienced on the spot.

When I'm in Russia, I travel alone as a matter of principle, war or no war. At the beginning of the present conflict, in September 1999, I applied for ad hoc accreditation as a war correspondent. When the Russians refused, I decided to cover the war from the Chechen side. I disguised myself as a Chechen woman, wrapping my body in layers of thick skirts, wool sweaters, and long scarves. Women are rarely noticed in Chechnya, and so I could be very discreet. People looked right through me or forgot I was there.

And being fluent in Russian, I had no need of a translator. This was a great advantage. Of course, I presented myself as a journalist to those I interviewed officially, but if I could avoid it, I didn't introduce myself at all. I simply watched and listened. I was able to move about freely, avoiding the organized junkets the Russian Army put on for the foreign press. Travelling alone, or with a Chechen friend to help me negotiate my way through the hundreds of highway checkpoints, I kept my mouth shut. When I encountered Russian soldiers, I remained expressionless or I feigned exhaustion, leaning my head against the dirty car window as I waited through yet another perfunctory border control. I learned to anticipate the behavior of the Russians on duty, to have a ready response to any emergency. I knew I could retrace my steps if necessary or reveal my identity and profession. Fortunately— and I had a lot of good fortune during these six months—I never once had to turn back. That being said, in the midst of a full-scale war, it is always too late to turn back or to hide, and so I stayed.

I lived through hell. I experienced the kind of fear that wipes out any other thought or feeling, that makes your mouth dry. I felt deep solidarity with dozens of anonymous individuals with whom I shared moments of raw horror and moments of pure joy. I felt the intense happiness of small, fleeting pleasures—a glass of hot, black tea; a glint of sun off the snow-capped mountains. But mostly I felt cold and tired after kilometers and kilometers of tramping along mountain roads or across open plains, by night, trying to cross through the Russian lines.

I kept going. Moving forward. Asking questions. I tried to meet as many people as possible; women and children whose lives had been destroyed by the war, rebel fighters with nothing left to lose, cynical Russian soldiers mired in an "anti-terrorist" operation whose success they doubted. What kept me going? The will to do my job, to never stop writing. It was my sense of myself as a journalist that allowed me to survive in Chechnya. Whenever I could, I reverted to my own little professional rite: I extracted my legal-size sheets of paper from the cheap plastic boots I'd bought at a Chechen market, smoothed them out with the flat of my hand, and began to write with my ballpoint pen whose ink often froze from the cold. I wrote for my French audience at home. I imagined them buying the paper the next day and scanning the headlines as they sipped their coffees in Parisian cafés. I revisited my own favorite cafés in my mind's eye. I imagined so hard that I could almost hear the grinding of the espresso machines, the clink of coffee cups, and the rustle of readers turning newspaper pages.

Then I filed my copy. Using my satellite telephone, speaking very slowly and distinctly, I would dictate my article to someone far away in France who jotted it down in shorthand. Once the dictation was over, I found little else to add. I had trouble chitchatting. What more could I say? Besides, I was always worried about running down the batteries in my telephone. I would have to find somewhere to recharge them, a car battery or a tractor engine.

As this book goes to press, the war in Chechnya persists. Blood, bombs, snipers, torture, and intimidation are wearing down both sides. Unfortunately, the conflict is far from over. Perhaps it will never end. Issues are not being addressed, much less resolved. And what are the "issues" anyway? So the painful story continues and I—and other writers and journalists—must return as witnesses to the scene. No one else will tell the truth.

I have been back to Chechnya several times since the writing of this book and I intend to repeat this exercise until the conflict ends. For me, who had only encountered stories of war through history books, Chechnya is a lesson in war's harsh reality—the cruelty, the despair, the boredom, the death. For the reader, I hope that these pages will help to untangle the series of events leading up to this tragedy. I have written this book to tell the pitiful and pointless story of war and to show the plight of a proud people, these Chechen men and women, with whom I bore the unbearable.

Chapter 1

"WATCH OUT for your bags. Don't leave them just anywhere. Given the current situation, you must be constantly on your guard, especially for cars. The terrorists use old ones, rather battered, so watch where you park."

The heavily made-up evening news broadcaster on the local Makhachkala* television is ticking off important points. As in Moscow, neighborhood patrols are organized to keep nightly watch over large apartment blocks. Still, you can't be too careful. Here, in the southern reaches of the Russian Federation, not far from Chechnya, fear pervades the atmosphere. In the short distance between the airport and the town center, I pass through no fewer than four checkpoints; at one of them, officials register my arrival.

---

* Makhachkala is the capital of Dagestan, Chechnya's neighboring republic in the Russian Federation.

I've flown in from Moscow to cover the Russian military's recent attacks on two villages in Dagestan. The Russians say they are defending Dagestan from invading Chechen rebels,* but I won't form an opinion until I've seen the villages and talked to the locals. I'm here to investigate and I will interview anyone who's willing to talk about what's going on.

Maimussat is the assistant director of the city opera, which was opened about a year ago, and she is worried about an impending war. "It's a commercial war," she says. "The people of Dagestan have no desire for war, but we're on the oil route, and our president is corrupt. He has had his eyes closed for a long time now. They say he's been bought by the terrorists; in exchange, he let them have an escape route [back to Chechnya] after the fifteen days' war."

I ask her about the Wahhabis.† She says she doesn't really know who they are, but because I need background information, she opens the window of her apartment in the center of town and calls to her son, Kamal: "Go get Amerbek. Tell him to come over for a visit; we'll have some tea. Yes, yes, right away."

---

* In August 1999, Chechen warlord Shamil Bassayev staged several incursions into neighboring Dagestan from Chechnya in the hopes of establishing an Islamic republic.

† Wahhabis are Muslim religious fundamentalists. In comparison to the majority Sufi Chechens (adherents of the traditional Chechen Muslim brotherhoods called *tariqats*), the Wahhabis are an extremist group who advocate an orthodox view of Islam and reject secular forms of government. The Wahhabi sect of Islam has grown in the former Soviet Union as a result of the relaxation of Soviet-era restrictions on religious proselytizing. It was brought into Chechnya mainly during the 1994–96 war. Wahhabis support independence for the mostly Muslim regions of the Caucasus.

Kamal takes the stairs four at a time and arrives out of breath. "Why do you want Amerbek? I don't even know where he is," he snaps, annoyed by his mother's sudden interest in one of his school friends.

"Because he's a Wahhabi," replies Maimussat, laughing.

That evening, a gangly adolescent turns up. We sit down among the cartons and rolled-up rugs in Maimussat's apartment, which is in the process of being renovated. With his arms crossed and resting on his knees, Amerbek begins to talk. Right before the bombings, he says, he stayed with his cousin in Karamakhi for fifteen days.

"Karamakhi and Chabanmakhi were two peaceful little villages where no one smoked or drank. Not like the rest of the world at all! Wahhabism was introduced there seven years ago. The inhabitants are poor, of course, but content. They live off potatoes down there," the young man explains gravely. "Now there's nothing left, not a house. The Federals* took everything—television sets, rugs—anything they could get their hands on."

Just before he rushes down the stairs with Kamal in tow, Amerbek asks me, "Is it true that the Muslims are the largest religion in the world?"

Moments later, Amerbek's mother, Uma, appears at the apartment in search of her son. Now it's her turn to talk. She has divided loyalties, because, although she is not Wahhabi, her husband's family is. She is passionate about the subject.

"There was much that was good in what I saw there, in the two

---

* Chechens call the Russian armed forces the "Federals."

villages. Burials lasted only three days and not seven; weddings there were simple, without music; relations between parents and children were not at all as they are here, where the young people talk back to their elders," she says, shaking her head and fingering the knot of the imitation Hermès scarf she wears around her neck.

"I am Muslim, but I am not inclined to cover my face, to see my husband grow a beard, and to have to pray five times a day, as they do down there," she adds.

⌂

The Hotel Leningrad is a short distance away, on Lenin Avenue. A few rusted umbrella stands, their fabric long since rotted away, decorate a sidewalk café, which is in ruins. A man is hosing down the sidewalk in front of this hovel. With the exception of the FSB* headquarters, which have recently been repainted, all the buildings on the street are peeling. The mayor's office is on the fifth floor of a Soviet-style building directly across the street from the local "White House."† In an antichamber, four men with pistols tucked in their belts are crouched in front of a television set. They appear to be mesmerized by a report on training camps for the Wahhabi forces in neighboring Chechnya. On the wall, an immense canvas in garish colors shows a jackal devouring a wolf; this against a background of the Caucasus mountains depicted with female faces.

---

* The FSB is Russia's Federal Security Service. It replaced the KGB after the collapse of the Soviet Union.
† Administrative seat of the republic.

Fabulous kitsch! The round little mayor, seated in a wheelchair—he has escaped many attempts on his life—has little to say: "The Chechens don't come around here because they know we detest them. They would have liked to turn us into an Islamic republic. Let them go to hell! The inhabitants of the two villages you're asking about resisted their assailants, who were armed to the teeth...."

He offers me a car and driver so that I can go and see these places for myself.

⌓

We drive through two mountain passes and along a series of steep roads winding their way around stark outcroppings of rock. At last we reach the two villages. Two years ago, local Wahhabis proclaimed them Muslim territory, subject to the rule of the *charia*.* The villages were reconquered by the Russian army in mid-September 1999, after two weeks of intensive pounding. To reach this short-lived Islamic minirepublic, one must first pass through Buinaksk, where, on September 4, the second in a series of bloody bombings was carried out by what Moscow terms "Caucasian terrorists." Sixty-four villagers lost their lives. In the center of town, the building that suffered the explosion is still standing, as though in defiance of the laws of gravity. On the outskirts are residential blocks, which were buffeted by the blast and are now shunned by locals as uninhabitable.

"The Russians are going to leave, for certain," Enver explains.

---

* Islamic law.

The twenty-two-year-old is loitering, bored, in the ruins. He may be right. For now, however, the Russians are still here. At each entrance and exit of the town, cars are stopped and checked by sullen Kalachnikov-armed soldiers or even, on occasion, by members of the OMON, the special forces of the Ministry of the Interior.

In the countryside, twenty kilometers further on, we encounter entire garrisons of Russians; they are lumbering along in decrepit army vehicles or marching through the dust back to one of their bases in what was once a Soviet farm. The carcasses of dead animals—cows, goats, horses—along the road suggest that we are not far from the two villages recently retaken by the Russians. As we round a bend in the road, we come upon four peasants engaged in raising the remains of two tanks from a ravine with a tractor and an improvised winch. The tank motors will fetch a good price in the market at Buinaksk.

On the ridge beyond a checkpoint, where Russian troops and Dagestani recruits stand guard against possible new incursions by Wahhabis or their Chechen acolytes, lie the ruins of Karamakhi village. Not one house has escaped the aerial bombardments of the Russian Federal Army. Roofs have collapsed; only the vestiges of walls remain standing. Here and there, one can guess at what was once a kitchen, a dining room, or a bedroom by a shred of wallpaper or an abandoned household object. The impact of the missiles has left craters in the midst of cabbage and potato fields. "It looks like a second Kuwait!" Nadyr, my driver, repeats over and over. Three large fellows from Dagenergo, the state electric company, are trying to get the system up and running. "Maybe this evening," one of them volunteers. He sounds doubtful.

In his ragged Marlboro T-shirt, Magomed gives us a tour of his "property." His three-story house has completely collapsed. Not a door left, not a stick of furniture, no television. Everything has disappeared, blown away by the Wahhabis or the Federals. Strolling through the ruins, Magomed rails at the world. "If Yeltsin had cleaned out the Kremlin three years ago, none of this would ever have happened." Magomed hasn't much more to say about Moscow's grand political designs. Since the attack by the Wahhabis and the retaking of their village by the Russian army, the inhabitants of Karamakhi and Chabanmakhi are confused. They don't understand what has happened, why they have been bombarded with such fury, or how they should go about rebuilding their lives.

A great ambiguity exists in the relations between Russia and this area and its inhabitants. The Russian army did come to the aid of Dagestan in its struggle against the "Wahhabi threat," but at what price?

"From the sky, the pilots couldn't know whether the house they were bombing was Wahhabi or not," Magomed insists. "But why did they have to destroy *everything*? That we'll never know. Moreover," he adds, "if they had really wanted to stop those Wahhabis, it would have been much simpler to go about it differently. Every Friday the Wahhabis got together at the mosque to pray. They could simply have rounded them up at the exits. Now, of course, they're dispersed all over the place."

Magomed knew the Wahhabis. They had taken up residence in the cellar of his house, which overlooked the village; then they dug trenches around the house and narrowed its large windows into gun slits. Strewn about the floor, among the paving stones and the damp earth, are ten or so syringes still in their original packing. Others, which have been used, have been thrown into a corner. "No doubt they had to raise their morale before battle," Magomed notes with a sneer.

Magomed's wife, Aminat, appears behind him out of the ruins. She is wearing tattered woolen tights and an old flowered tunic; a colored scarf is knotted around her neck. Aminat gives full vent to her sorrow: "For twenty-five years, we saved our kopecks so we could build this house. Now we've lost everything. On the first day of the bombing, even before it began, the rumor circulated that war was going to break out. Everybody said, 'It's time to leave.' We ran off with just the clothes on our backs, nothing else." The attack began that evening.

In this ghostly village empty of residents, the story of Magomed and Aminat is repeated over and over again. The men return in the mornings from Buinaksk and other neighboring areas to continue clearing the ruins and to try to rescue some of their possessions. Women and children generally stay in whatever improvised shelter they found after "the events," either with parents or friends, or in one of the two camps opened for them in Buinaksk. Few women have the courage to come back to dig about in the earth for a few potatoes, as Aminat does. In the village center, on a dusty square with a battered administration building, general confusion reigns, born of the villagers' comings

and goings, their furtive conversations, and the maneuverings of
the enormous Kamaz dump trucks, which carry the debris away.
Activity is greatest on the field of ruins where men, trowels and
bricks in hand, have already begun the work of reconstruction.

"That is our old mosque," murmurs Ibadulla Mukhaev, a former employee of the municipality. Rolled rugs lie about in the
dirt. "This war has absolutely nothing to do with religion," he
explains. "It has to do, first and foremost, with political machina-
tions. We have been the innocent victims. You certainly don't need
arms to pray."

Several kilometers further along, on the flank of another hill,
lie the ruins of Chabanmakhi. An armed group stationed at the
entrance to the village refuses access to all visitors.

"Orders," a guard assures me. He does not wear a uniform, but
his manner is menacing, and he cradles a machine gun across his
chest. We wait. At last, a small man emerges from the group, iden-
tifies himself as the "new administrator" of the village, and
declares that he alone has the right to decide who may or may not
come in. Voices are raised; eventually, the guards allow my car to
enter.

Here, again, the devastation is total. The village is less densely
settled, but no house has escaped the shelling. At the end of the
dirt path leading to the top of the village, an old man in a worn-
out suit stands facing the panorama.

"I was born in this village seventy-five years ago," he tells me.
"We knew the Wahhabis here. Almost every family was mixed;
sometimes a father would be Wahhabi but not his son or vice
versa. For years now they have prevented the sale of cigarettes and

alcohol in the village. For two years, we've had no federal law in this small area."

"In particular," another chimes in, "they forbade us to decorate Christmas trees at the end of the year or to play music at our weddings. At funerals, crying was frowned upon; our women had to hold back their tears."

"In fact, we didn't really bother each other," the old man continues. "If only they'd held the nation [the Soviet Union] together, none of this would have happened. No one from abroad would have given them money; they wouldn't have been able to procure arms so easily or take power little by little at our expense," he laments.

In the middle of a field, beside the cemetery, yawns a common grave. I note the remains of fourteen Wahhabis, no doubt abandoned by their fleeing comrades. By the light of the setting sun, the inhabitants of the village have begun to inter the dead. They scatter shovelsful of earth over the heap of rotting bodies. Other forgotten corpses lie here and there in the surrounding potato field, awaiting burial.

As darkness settles on Karamakhi and Chabanmakhi, it's time to leave the high ground and return to the relative safety of the valley below.

"At night, the Wahhabis do what we do during the day. They come up here to see what's going on, to try to recover what they can of their belongings. After all, it was their village, too," Zapir Chikhchabekov, a young administrator from Chabanmakhi, concludes bitterly.

I must find a bus leaving for Vladikavkaz in North Ossetia, or for Nazran in Ingushetia.* It is the evening of September 29, 1999, and the Federal troops are getting ready for an invasion of Chechen territory on the morning of October 1.† If I want to witness the deployment, I'll have to move fast. All buses travelling west from Makhachkala must make an enormous detour around the perimeter of Chechnya. The trip will take twenty-two hours.

The night air is still warm. The driver stops repeatedly for routine checks at MVD‡ posts, or to pick up passengers or merchandise by the side of the road. After all, he has to make a little extra to top off his monthly salary of 250 rubles;** he can take in ten times that amount in one night alone. Women are traveling with large cargo shipments of "salmon," which is code for merchandise, I am told discreetly. Should they run into trouble with the law, women are apparently better able to argue their cases than men are.

Around 2:30 A.M., traveling close to the Chechen border, the bus makes a longer stop than usual, this one near a militia post. Eventually, the customs agents set about searching the cargo and discover six hundred kilos of contraband. The women cry and

---

* North Ossetia and Ingushetia are two other republics in the Russian Federation. Ingushetia lies between North Ossetia and Chechnya. I often had to cross through Ingushetia and its capital, Nazran, on my way into Chechnya from North Ossetia. Please see map.

† Russia had been bombing Chechnya for several weeks. Air raids began on September 5. The Russians claimed they were trying to liberate Chechnya from the grip of international terrorists.

‡ Russian Ministry of the Interior.

** $165.

plead with the head of the militia, who maintains a calm demeanor under his bulletproof vest. With their high heels sinking deep into the mire, they swarm around him, pulling at his sleeve. He affects incomprehension. This little comedy goes on for two hours, but it's a well-rehearsed drama, in which all the actors are to be rewarded: The militiaman is "recompensed," the bus driver as well, and the women, each one several bank notes lighter, are allowed to continue on their way.

Inside the bus, everyone is more or less awake. A few of the passengers are annoyed by the delay and don't hesitate to say so. In the seat in front of mine, an imposing woman with round glasses and her hair tied back in an old-fashioned bun makes no bones about her displeasure. "And what about us?" she hollers. "What are we supposed to be doing while you're all making money? Damned bus, let's go...." Her shouting is met with silence from the others.

In the early hours of the morning, in the Republic of Kabardino-Balkaria* not far away from Ingushetia, we run into a milk-like fog. "It will lift," my Dagestani neighbor assures me. He is a former chauffeur of Communist dignitaries, now on his way to visit his mother in Vladikavkaz. We cross the immense and murky Terek River on a pontoon bridge, a large prefabricated iron platform floating on top of the water. I am told that, to get to Nazran, I must change buses immediately. The driver lets me off in the middle of nowhere. "Over there," he tells me. "Wait for the next bus, the one turning right." It's 8:00 A.M., and foggy; I can't see a thing.

---

* A republic neighboring Chechnya in the Russian Federation.

A stooped black form is approaching in the mist. A woman stag-
gering under the weight of two heavy bags, one in each hand, joins
me. She assures me that a bus will indeed come along "before
noon." Her eyes are slanted, her features Asian.

"My grandparents were Korean," Alifat tells me. She is on her
way to peddle medicines in a nearby village in Ingushetia. "I lived
my whole life in Chechnya, and we lived rather well. My husband
worked as a mason in those days. But we left right after the first
war* because life became unbearable for non-Chechens like us.
Now war is going to break out again, for sure."

Alifat is so involved in her story that we miss the bus. It barrels
along at a high speed, passing right under our noses. I run after it
frantically. Alifat is beside herself; her day is ruined.

Blinded at this hour of the morning by the sun which has broken through the fog and now glints off the yellow steppe, we
hadn't noticed another woman approaching. She wears a scarf tied
around her wrinkled face. Rosa is a Russian, born in Kabardia.
"There will be another bus, but for Novy Redant, not for
Nazran," she explains. When? "Before noon." From my position
at the side of the road, I stick my arm out, hoping to stop a passing car and commandeer it as a taxi, as they do in Moscow. "Don't

---

* The earlier war between Russia and Chechnya took place between 1994 and
  1996. Chechnya gained de facto independence after inflicting heavy losses on
  Russian forces.

even bother," the two locals insist. "You don't know the Kabardino-Balkars. They would never stop. You're wasting your time." It's true. Though the passing cars don't appear to be full, no one stops for us.

This time we won't let it pass us by! A rusted minibus with no indication of its destination comes to a stop just as we are rising from the grass where we've been having a quiet chat. We climb aboard and remain standing, as there are no seats left. Total silence. The bus is full of sullen-looking people on their way to work. After ten minutes, Alifat gives me a nudge: It's time to get off. The surrounding landscape is even more deserted here than at the previous crossroads. As the bus pulls away toward its mystery destination, the three of us strike out on a dirt path, walking straight into the sun. The majestic Caucasus with their impenetrable shadows rise up before us.

"Where are we going?" I ask.

"We're going to cross the frontier into Ingushetia," they tell me.

A silence falls upon us as we walk on. I am in the center of our trio, and take on some of the weight of their bundles in addition to my backpack. We never seem to get any closer to the mountains, and there is no frontier post visible ahead. Nothing but yellow and blue around us. I just have to trust my two little old guides.

At a turning in the path, I at last spy a lookout post down below and a red-and-white gate, similar to a level crossing for the railroad. We can't yet make it out clearly, but a large immobile crowd appears to gather on the far side of a second gate.

We are the only ones passing from the Balkar side into Ingushetia. The young officer who looks over our papers pales when he catches sight of my French passport. He speaks into his walkie-talkie: "I have a foreigner here. What in the hell is she doing here? What am I supposed to do with her?" he asks his boss.

"I'm traveling around, visiting Russia on foot. Don't I have the right?" I answer in Russian, which makes him go paler still. After half an hour of palaver, the guards, who are at a loss, allow me to cross. I rejoin my two companions, who are waiting for me with the crowd on the other side.

In the background, on the horizon, lies the snow-covered summit of Mount Kazbek, which marks the frontier with Georgia. In front of us we see a column of cars, full of women and children, crossing the vast plain—more Chechens coming to join those who are already waiting to cross into Ingushetia. The crowd at the gate has been waiting more than twenty-four hours.

Zarima stands out in the crowd. She has long black hair held back with a band, and she's wearing denim overalls and high heels. She must be about thirty years old. She describes her personal situation in a monotone: "The Chechens are now hated everywhere. How do you expect our children to grow up? And it's all because a band of madmen went to make war in Dagestan!" She motions toward her three children, aged six, five, and three, who accompany her: "My only concern is their education. When it comes down to it, it's probably better to leave, because I've had enough of seeing children grow up with Kalachnikovs."

Seda, elegant in a long black dress, a scarf covering her head and large Christian Dior glasses dominating her pale oval face, is unmarried and childless, unusual in this part of the world. She is a law student in the Chechen capital, Grozny, but she can no longer pursue her studies at the university, which closed its doors after the air strikes began.

"We're no longer afraid that we'll be killed," she explains solemnly. "It's the waiting that's become intolerable. What will happen tomorrow? Who's in charge of our government? When will the land war begin? No one can answer these questions, so we must leave. My dream is to get to Moscow and continue my studies, but I know it won't be possible, simply because I'm a Chechen."

Eventually, we flag down a car that takes us to a village where we go our separate ways. I wind up on a bus bound for Nazran. Women and young girls are crammed cheek by jowl in this stuffy space. The schoolgirls wear uniforms from another era, little black skirts and white lace aprons crisscrossing their chests.

Everyone on the bus seems worried about the situation. They're eager to talk. An old woman is ranting in Russian, for my obvious benefit: "And Bassayev,* that criminal. He should have been arrested long ago.... It's only because he's in cahoots with the Russians...."

We pass other buses, which are also full of refugees moving about from village to village.

---

* Shamil Bassayev, Moscow's "number-one terrorist," is one of the principal leaders in the Chechen battle for independence.

"They go from house to house. People sometimes take them in if they have children with them," a woman tells me.

"They also sleep and cook in abandoned cars," another woman adds.

≙

Nazran, the capital of Ingushetia, is flat and colorless. The city is small because until 1992, the Soviet Socialist Republic of Chechno-Ingushetia, which combined the two geographical entities, had Grozny as its capital. As a result, Nazran looks like any Chechen town; it's comprised mainly of one-story brick houses, with a few larger, two-story dwellings for the more prosperous.

The border with Chechnya lies thirty kilometers to the east. For a week now, tens of thousands of Chechens have been leaving their homes in a continuous flow because they fear the outbreak of another war between their country and the Russian Federation. Between Chechnya and Ingushetia, a never-ending column of vehicles—dusty BMWs, noisy Ladas, and cattle trucks—creep along under a warm autumn sun.

Swamped by the scale of the migration, the Ingushetia border guards make almost no effort to check documents. Despite their Kalachnikovs and their army uniforms, they serve more as traffic cops than as a police force.

A first refugee camp has been hastily set up beside the road. It consists of about a hundred yellow army tents and a medical center where basic drugs are available. Twice a day, the police distribute water and bread.

"Officially, 3,500 people live here, but that's not counting those who haven't registered, and there are many of them," Abdullah Karamekh, a representative of the Ingush government, tells me. As director of the camp, he deals every day with distraught mothers and grandmothers struggling to explain the chaos in their households.

Sitting cross-legged on a bit of cardboard in the shade of an enormous Kamaz truck wheel, a refugee named Aizan tries to make a little money in this unpromising environment. When she left the Chechen capital, Grozny, Aizan brought the leftover stock of her little kiosk—some socks, a couple of bottles of shampoo, a few pieces of soap, and some cigarettes. A circle has formed around the truck, suggesting that her improvised business is doing well. "But I've been obliged to lower my prices," she laments, "because everyone here is so poor."

There is a continuous bustle around her. Women are doing laundry or struggling to cook a few potatoes acquired on the run. The men fill their hours with random tasks—moving a truck, say, or searching for someone in authority. Meanwhile, children here are half shocked, half amused to find themselves living in open country, under tents, while they wait for their parents to decide the family's next move.

"It's Putin* who's the terrorist," a man says loudly. "Thanks to us, since we're all leaving, his popularity is on the rise." When I question him further, he admits that Chechen President Aslan

---

* Vladimir Putin, then prime minister of the Russian Federation. Putin is currently president of the Russian Federation.

Maskhadov and the warlord Shamil Bassayev also share responsibility for the forced exodus of the population. Then he lowers his voice so that the others cannot overhear him: "In fact, we're really at a dead-end. No one is looking out for us. Others are deciding our fate. They are making us wander the world like Gypsies."

Only little Ingushetia (population: 300,000) has agreed to accept the refugees. Historically, Chechnya and Ingushetia have always been close. They share a similar language and, until 1992, they belonged to the same republic. During the first Chechen war in 1994, the Ingush rose up several times against the Russian forces, even crossing into neighboring Chechnya to defend their border. This time, their sense of solidarity is weaker. "Of course, we ought to take in the refugees, and many Ingush have taken in Chechens out of a feeling of fraternity, but our people are tired of living with these historical ups and downs," explains Ruslan Tchakhaev, vice president of the migration service in the Nazran mayor's office.

Here in the capital of Ingushetia, refugees are everywhere. They've invaded every public place, every administrative center, and every railway station. They're sleeping on the ground or on rugs and mattresses they've been able to salvage. They wander from village to village in the hope of finding work or a roof over their heads, if only for a night.

Without the least hesitation, I set off for Grozny. I leave Nazran in the early hours of the morning. I have strapped my most prized possession, my satellite phone, to my belly. It will be my only means to reach Moscow. I'll dictate my reports over the phone. I've chosen my disguise carefully. I am wearing a long navy blue dress with white polka dots, and a scarf is tied around my neck. I want to look just like a Chechen woman. I want to disappear into crowds. Of my normal wardrobe, I have kept only my socks and walking shoes.

I am alone in the car with a man called Aslan, whom I barely know; but he is a friend of my friend Igor, in whom I have complete confidence. Seated behind Aslan in a green Lada, I'll appear to be the wife of the driver. Here, women never sit in the front seat of a car.

Aslan is a twenty-nine-year-old Chechen banker who has lived in Moscow for the last ten years. As we head for the Chechen border, he gives me a warning: "Nothing has changed there since the end of the first war; nothing has been rebuilt. Almost all the schools are closed. Life there has become impossible. No one talks to anyone else or exchanges visits. What has become of our traditional hospitality? Those who take journalists or others hostage are bandits who do it for the ransom. The fact is that these operations are planned undercover by the Russian special forces."*

Concerning Dagestan: "No Muslim state should be built on the blood of other Muslims! You won't find that anywhere in the Koran!" he cries between two choruses of his favorite song, "Living in America," which plays continuously on his tape deck.

---

* Kidnappings are very common in Chechnya. Journalists, Russians, and foreigners such as aid workers have been kidnapped on numerous occassions by various groups operating in the region.

Aslan has agreed to make a round-trip to Grozny, where he has "some business to attend to." He is wanted in Moscow, and can no longer show his face there. Several months ago, grenades and various other prohibited weapons were discovered in his car. He says that Russian "agencies" planted the suspicious material in his trunk to create a pretext for his arrest. He has already paid $60,000 in bribes to lawyers and various judicial bodies in an effort to end the affair; this is what keeps him "waiting" in one of the two suites of Nazran's only hotel.

At Sleptsovskii, a border town, a young man climbs into the car and takes his place beside Aslan. This is Islam, a twenty-four-year-old former soldier, whom I met during the previous Chechen war. He has agreed to serve as my guide while I'm here investigating.

No problems crossing the border. At this time, early October 1999, everything is still open; anyone can come into Chechnya. At the checkpoint, Islam gets out of the car and has a word with the sentry on duty, who wears a Colt revolver stuck in his belt. The sentry signals us to move ahead, and we pass all the other waiting cars. We carry on at a fast clip. There is little traffic in our direction, but a stream of packed convoys is heading the other way, toward the safety of Ingushetia.

≙

Although the first Russian armored divisions entered Chechen territory two days earlier, here in the Chechen capital the atmosphere seems strangely calm. Outside the city, a giant petrol refinery stands out in stark, metallic relief, blackened in a recent fire caused by the Russian bombardment. It was designated a strategic target and heavily bombed in 1994, at the start of the first Russo-Chechen war. Now it has been destroyed again. Big, gaudy bath towels imprinted with the U.S. flag hang between the trees, flapping in the wind. At the entrance to Grozny, the GAI* station is barely recognizable amidst the rubble and the sandbags; a shell found its mark here last week. Women are carrying pails of water. Everywhere people are selling cans of *salionka*, a poor-quality gasoline. The town is a patchwork of tumbled-down buildings and small makeshift constructions barely distinguishable from the ruins around them. Three old men, seated on their doorstep, are chatting quietly. With a leafy branch, a woman vigorously shoos the flies away from her stall of raw, bloody meat.

In the northeastern section of town, on Ingushetskaya Street, a cluster of four houses with brick walls and pointed roofs has also fallen victim to the Russian assault. In the early morning mist, roosters crow loudly to one another. Squatting on what remains of their roofs, a couple of men try to size up their losses. I hear a creaking sound as an old woman pushes open a blue metal door decorated with a symmetrical white design. She steps out of her courtyard and heads toward two scrawny cows grazing in the dry mud. When she closes the door behind her, I notice the pockmarks of fifteen or so shell fragments on its decorative motif.

Maaka doesn't try to hide her anger. "Of course, they're killing innocent victims," she declares as she scowls up at the sky, the

---

* Traffic police.

source of so much destruction. "We saw it with our own eyes several days ago. They bombed right here. An entire family was killed, six people." It was a direct hit on the house next door. "I'm scared, too," she admits, "but what can you do? I can't leave; I simply have nowhere to go. And if they're going to bomb us, we can't do anything about it."

As we approach the center of town, the same scenes of mass destruction unfold before us. Windowless, gutted buildings are everywhere. We can tell from the bits of colored fabric at the windows that some of them are still inhabited. It is hard to distinguish between the damage of the first war and more recent hits. Even the locals have a hard time remembering. They almost always hesitate for a moment when they answer questions about the dates of their losses.

In the town center, on the former Lenin Square, now rebaptized Liberty Square, an attractive and shady park has appeared on the spot formerly occupied by the residence of Dzhokhar Dudayev, the first Chechen leader to fight for the complete independence of his country from the Soviets. Russians razed the house in 1994. Now a huge billboard of a smiling Dudayev appears over the tops of the greenery, the only bit of novelty introduced here since 1996. All the damaged buildings from the first war have been left as they were, riddled with shell holes or lying crumpled in ruins. Nothing has been rebuilt. A few red or white brick houses, such as the imposing home of Shamil Bassayev's brother and the majestic residence of the current president, Aslan Maskhadov, have gone up. Mercedes with tinted windows and jeeps bearing the green, white, and red stickers of

"Ichkeria"* are parked here and there. There are hardly any stores; electricity is rare; there is no hot water; and telephone communication was cut off five years ago. In the street, men are preoccupied with repairing cars for their journey to the Ingushetia frontier, the goal of most of the refugees. At the end of the Avenue of the Revolution, in the middle of a traffic circle, stands a statue of three soldiers of the Russian revolution, renamed "The Three Idiots" by local residents. Their eyes, noses, and mouths have been hammered out.

Only the open-air market functions twenty-four hours a day. Men with beards and wearing camouflage scurry about, cellular or satellite phones clipped to their belts or glued to their ears. A hoarse voice, speaking Russian, announces into a microphone the results of the lottery. Behind the displays of tomatoes and cucumbers, next to the quarters of beef and veal at the butchers' stands, we find the arms market. Women are not welcome here. To kill time—because buying a Kalachnikov takes quite a bit of it—the men play billiards. All, young and old alike, argue endlessly with the *boyviki*.† In a corner, a crowd gathers around munitions displays: piles of Russian-made grenades of varying quality, grenade-launchers in a variety of calibers, ammunition by the hundredweight, and pistols to suit all needs.

"When war seemed less likely, several months ago, prices were relatively low," Aslanbek, an arms seller, explains. "Then every-

---

* The pro-independents' name for Chechnya.
† The Russian word for combatants; the name the Russians have given to the pro-independence Chechens.

one started wanting personal arms, and they began to rise. Now they've gone back down again." Apparently, everyone has already acquired his weapon of choice. Sales are down. In August 1999, a Kalachnikov cost $900; today it's worth $500. Grenades are $2 apiece. An automatic grenade-launcher fetches about $1,000. Before finalizing a sale, the buyers try out the weapons. And so the days go by, punctuated by the crack of trial shots fired in the air.

After visiting the stands where real arms are sold, I wander among the stalls devoted to plastic pistols and other children's toys. Nearby are the "changers," a cocky-looking group, standing about casually with bundles of bills in their hands.

⌂

Umar, twenty-five years old, grew up in the 1980s in the Soviet Republic of Checheno-Ingushetia and served in the first Russo-Chechen War; he is now preparing himself for the outbreak of another conflict and asking himself what his life might have been like without these wars. "Ichkeria's" independence seems to concern the population less than the commercial interests that have once again brought war to the Caucasus. This former *boyvik*, whose upper lip has been smashed by a bullet, has no confidence in any of the Chechen leaders. "One thing is certain: Aslan Maskhadov doesn't have 1 percent control of the situation. He can't even name his ministers or remove them," he tells me.

We're sitting in the Meridian Café in Grozny. Umar is flattered when I ask him to give his opinion on the political impasse in which the independent republic of Chechnya now finds itself, and to explain the roles of the various armed groups that control his country. He is also proud to demonstrate that in this devastated city—where, in recent years, numerous foreigners have been kidnapped and murdered solely for ransom money—there are some tranquil spots where one can pretend to live normally. He continuously underscores this theme, with obvious satisfaction, during our discussion.

The "café" is actually just a private apartment transformed into a dive. Three badly dyed blondes are working in the kitchen. The two other rooms resemble a private home, with a couch, a table, some chairs, and a television set. The Meridian opened after the first war, early in 1997. "You can find this sort of little café all over Grozny," Umar explains proudly. "And one eats very well here." Most of the customers are armed men who have enough money to treat themselves to a "European-style" lunch or dinner; that is, a relatively copious meal.

Today, facing yet another war, Umar is more worried about the growing power of the Wahhabis than he is about the internal struggles at the top of the Chechen power elite. He is the head of a band, or what Moscow calls a "terrorist group." His troops, comprised of his family and of other men from his geographic area, control the northwest sector of Grozny up to the border with Ingushetia.

"My role is to prevent any provocation between the Wahhabis and the Russian forces who are approaching," he explains, as he plays idly with the strap attaching his Beretta to his belt. "The other day, a Wahhabi leader came to see me to urge me to enlist on their side in the Jihad, the holy war. 'The Russians are already nearby, it's getting dangerous,' he told me; 'we should attack them ourselves.' I told him that it was out of the question." He looks up at me quizzically and takes a sip of hot tea from a porcelain cup. "The Russians say that their first priority is to wipe out the Wahhabis, but oddly enough, the Wahhabi base at Urus-Martan has never been bombed."

Umar knows the Wahhabis well because the territory controlled by his 1,500-member band includes their base. Moreover, he had to deal with them when the heads of four missing persons —three Britons and a New Zealander—were discovered one fine morning by the side of the road.

"They were the ones who killed them!" he tells me. "I know it because these foreigners, who were working in our area, were under our protection. Suddenly, one night, they were taken. The next day, we kidnapped a Wahhabi. We wanted to exchange him for the four Anglo-Saxons. But their chief [he won't say the name] refused. He would have preferred that we kill his man rather than release the four foreigners. It turned nasty. In the end they executed their prisoners," he sighs. The reprisals must have been brutal, but when I ask, Umar refuses to elaborate.

"That said, not all the men who wear beards in our country are Wahhabis," he says, changing the subject. "True Wahhabis shave their mustaches. And the custom is for them to pull three hairs out of their beards every day, out of superstition. Wahhabism came to us out of Dagestan. Until very recently there wasn't a trace

of it around here," he insists, explaining that Islamic fundamentalism appeared in Chechenya only "after the war"; that is, after the
Khasavyurt accords, signed in August 1996.*

"Here, everybody treats us like dogs," he continues. "Including
the Wahhabis, who have no concern for our future." In his opinion, Shamil Bassayev and his Arab commander, Khattab, chose
the wrong faith. The world should "distinguish between those
who are ready to die for their religious beliefs and others who, like
Bassayev, corrupt to the core, would use these religious fanatics for
their own ends." Having said this, Umar suddenly looks sad. "If,
outside of Chechnya, no one supported Bassayev, he would have
no influence at all. Shamil is completely financially dependent on
the Wahhabis. In any case, he's a special agent who works only for
himself, not for the people of Chechnya."

The other prominent political figure, President Aslan
Maskhadov, democratically elected in January 1997, also finds no
favor with him. "We made a mistake when we elected Maskadov,"
Umar concedes. "He, too, is hand and glove with the Russian
secret service. We need a president who won't sell our country
cheap. A president who's capable of entering into real relations
with Russia."

According to Umar, the only way the Chechens will survive is
by organizing themselves as "individual princelings reigning over
their individual kingdoms. Each of them protects his own little
fief." And though he's a fighter, Umar prays every day that the "big

---

* Accords establishing a cease-fire between the Chechens and the Russians. They
were followed by a peace accord in May 1997.

war" will not start again. "When the Russian troops left in 1997, they were replaced by the special services, who introduced another, much more vicious, form of war," he laments. "They tried to buy everyone, to set us one against the other. Their goal was to devour us, little by little, from the inside, and just look at the result."

Is Umar blasé? Not really. It hurts him to contemplate his own future. "We'll see if I'm able to find a way out," he murmurs, his eyes downcast. "I had, in fact, plans for the kind of life I wanted to lead, but I haven't been able to act on them. And now, as far as the rest of the world is concerned, I'm a bandit." His voice assumes a touch of aggressiveness: "But that's not true, I'm not a bandit! I'm a man of my word. I'm defending my country. And even if, inside, I have the feeling that this second war won't happen, I have a burning sensation in my stomach that grows and grows whenever I think of it...."

In the street, two women are chatting quietly under the striped parasols of a shady sidewalk café. Their chairs are made of red plastic. In front of the central market, the cars, caught up in a traffic jam, inch slowly forward. Umar sets off on foot.

☖

As we leave Grozny, we pass through the village of Mitchurino, in the suburbs. There I meet Daud, an old man who is resting on a moth-eaten sofa in the courtyard of his house. Daud thinks carefully before he speaks. From time to time, he passes his hand over his *piess*, his gray prayer hat with royal blue embroidery, or stuffs the hem of his dark red shirt back into his checked trousers. He is so thin that he seems to float inside his clothes. Daud was born in a mountain village on the Georgian border, and worked for twenty-five years as a veterinarian in Grozny. He now receives a monthly pension of 1,100 rubles ($45). Although he was decorated for courage in service with the Russian army in World War II, he was nonetheless deported to Kazakhstan in 1944, by order of Stalin.* As soon as his rehabilitation was declared, he returned to Chechnya, and he means to never leave again. "When conditions are the most difficult, a real patriot makes a point of staying put. So I won't be going," he says fiercely. His wife, Zima, who is twenty years his junior, has left already for Sleptsovskii, in Ingushetia, two miles from the Chechen border.

"I'm ashamed for Western Europe, where you live in a world of lies. In the twenties, Russian terrorists were everywhere. Those are the ones you should have deported," he says in his weak nasal voice, which trails off into a sigh. "I'm already old; I've already done combat. It will be hard for me to fight again, but my machine gun is beside my bed, and if the Russians come and invade my house, I'll use it. Our problem is an absence of leaders. Dzhokhar† is dead, and no one has taken his place. Maskhadov and all the others you hear about in the West, none of them has any power. We are all victims, manipulated by the politicians in Moscow."

Most of the men I meet in Chechnya share this opinion.

---

* In 1944, Stalin deported many groups, including much of the Chechen population, to central Asia and Siberia on the pretext that they had collaborated with the enemy.
† Dzhokhar Dudayev, was killed in April 1996 by a Russian rocket. He was targeted by means of the satellite phone he was using at the time.

Chapter 2

AFTER A WEEK of traveling around Chechnya, gathering interviews, I return to my starting point, Vladikavkaz, the capital of North Ossetia. At the Ingushetia frontier, Russian soldiers are waiting in army vehicles, having returned from their "positions." The atmosphere at the checkpoint is visibly more tense than it was a week ago.

At Fifty-Eighth Army headquarters in the Ossetian capital, the soldiers are killing time. Sergei Marzoyev, a Russian officer, is lounging in his empty office. "Feeding our soldiers is no problem. Supporting their families is another story," he grumbles, referring to the small part of the national budget now devoted to the military. An attack of spleen overtakes him. "And what is this nonsense about international aid for a country of murderers? As for the Ingushetis, they're much too given to sentimentality. I don't see any signs of humanitarian disaster around here." Sergei is in his thirties. He has a round face, expressive eyebrows, and a crew-cut. He's angry, and he reminds me that a soldier's job is "making war." It's not his fault if this mandate is sometimes accompanied by atrocities.*

To make his point, he turns on his VCR. Twenty-five minutes of unbearable images follow. It's a videocassette of anti-Chechen propaganda showing, for example, the Chechens cutting off the fingers and ears of their prisoners before slitting their throats. "These scenes were filmed by the Chechens, who sent them on to their victims' families," Sergei thunders triumphantly. The Russians have added their own commentary to the clips, and the video has been sent to the Federation Council[†] in the hopes of persuading members to put the Chechen question to rest once and for all.

I protest, "But these films are from the first war with Chechnya!"

"It makes no difference," Sergei answers. "It's all starting up again. We're up to our necks in it already."

Like most military men, Sergei has no great love for journalists, especially those who don't offer to pay for information. He agrees, finally, to allow me to accompany his men to Mazdok, on the nothern tip of Ossetia, several kilometers from the frontier with Chechnya. There I will receive an accreditation from the

---

* There are extensive reports detailing the cycle of torture, extortion, and other human rights abuses faced by thousands of Chechens whom Russian forces have detained in Chechnya.
† The upper chamber of the Russian parliament.

Russian military allowing me to cover what the Kremlin linguists call their "Operation Antiterrorist." The accreditation will be issued by the headquarters of the Federal forces of the Northern Caucasus.

At dawn the next day, the "clubcar"* is ready. Two soldiers—a driver and an aide—have been assigned to go to Mozdok† to fetch a group of entertainers and bring them back to Vladikavkaz to cheer up the tired troops. Our vehicle is armored and appears prehistoric. Inside, there is a ragged movie screen half unrolled and two ancient projectors mounted on metal tripods that clang together at each curve in the road. Sergei has had the grace to include a broken down armchair "for the comfort of the young lady."

Because we have been forbidden to take the direct route through Ingushetia, it will take us more than three hours to reach Mozdok. To avoid ambushes by the "bandits," the army has been ordered to skirt problem areas; every trip therefore takes that much longer. We pass military housing "constructed seven years ago by a German firm," the driver comments. The housing complex is encircled by barbed wire; laundry is drying on the windowsills.

Suddenly the van comes to an abrupt stop. We've reached the border with Kabardino-Balkaria. The VAI‡ inspector interrogates the two soldiers. It turns out that neither Piotr, the young conscript who is driving, nor Arkadi, the lieutenant who is accompa-

---

* A Russian army vehicle equipped with a movie screen.
† Headquarters of the Russian forces in the North Caucasus (North Ossetia).
‡ Military traffic police.

nying him (a blond boy with his cap on crooked) has bothered to bring his identity papers or even a driver's license. Arkadi, with his hands clasped behind his neck, appears embarrassed. He enters into a seemingly endless discussion with the VAI officer in charge.

"If I let you pass, I'm taking a big risk. Even though my retirement pay will amount to almost nothing, I just can't take that kind of chance," the officer declares.

"But we have a pass. We're on our way to pick up entertainers for the troops," Arkadi repeats weakly. He's botched his assignment and senses punishment in his future. Eventually, the men reach a compromise: A deputy from the checkpoint police will accompany us to the next village, Elkhotovo, where the young soldiers will be able to telephone their base and explain their predicament. This checkpoint has no means of communication with the outside world. "That's the army for you," Arkadi says with a sigh.

When we get to Elkhotovo, Arkadi disappears. Piotr naps, his head leaning on the steering wheel. Two hours later, Arkadi reappears with a paper in his hand, and we set off again. The problem seems to be resolved.

Several kilometers further on, we come upon a sheet-metal truck bearing the inscription "Wagon-Restaurant" parked by the side of the road. I invite the two soldiers to lunch because I know their salaries would never permit them such a luxury. They accept without a word, almost without enthusiasm, although I can tell that they're both as hungry as bears. The wrinkled face of an old woman appears behind a dirty window. We order borscht. Scratchy music begins to play in the background.

Arkadi tells me that he was posted to Vladikavkaz after the

events of August 1999 in Dagestan. "But it couldn't be calmer here," he adds hastily, in the hope of convincing me that the Russians have the situation under control. At the other end of a long wooden table set up alongside the van, two Kalmuk truckers slurp their soup. They cast furtive glances at our curious threesome. Then, having realized that I am not Russian, they send kind little smiles my way.

In Mozdok, the press headquarters are about as big as a closet. A television set, a computer, and two tables take up the whole room. The chief carefully examines the permit I have received from the Ministry of Foreign Affairs and promptly refuses to grant me accreditation: "You're a foreigner. No foreigner has ever received accreditation. The FSB have got to know the people who work in this area," he explains, nodding his head for emphasis. "Go," he adds, laconically. "And, by the way, how did you get in?"

"Through the door," I reply, "like everybody else, I suppose. But may I ask you some questions before I leave?"

Stanislav Firsov, a little disconcerted perhaps by this approach, agrees to indulge me. No doubt he is pleased to be the center of attention of a member of the foreign press.

I ask him how many losses the Russians and Chechens suffered in the early days of October. "I can't tell you precisely. We don't give out such information to nonaccredited journalists," he replies, visibly ill at ease. I can draw from him only the official line: "We wouldn't have attacked Chechnya if the Chechens hadn't committed aggressions against Dagestan. This is an antiterrorist operation, as its name implies. In the areas where we are present, we have endeavored to carry on talks. The military is playing a diplomatic role. That's all there is to say."

The friendly NCO who accompanies me to the door would like to give me his telephone number so that we could stay in touch, but instead he whispers to me, "I've been waiting for two years for this damned line. What a waste of time! The army is so poor that they can't even provide us with telephone service."

☐

This morning the fog is particularly thick. It's as if a heavy stage curtain had begun to rise but got stuck halfway up. We're in the mountains. In the far distance a steep summit gleams above the fog. The car skids around a curve. We turn our backs on this panorama and carry on in the opposite direction, towards Chechnya. This time, we're heading for the front. I haven't taken the trouble to dress as a Chechen woman; I hope my laziness won't prove fatal.

Aslan is back at the wheel. Today he's driving a red Niva.* When we reach the Sleptsovskii border, Islam is waiting for us. He has a pistol in his belt and a easy stride; he looks like a wild animal alert to danger, but at the same time, like a little kid. He places a Kalachnikov beside me on the back seat of the car; it's an accessory I am already pretty familiar with. The scene would amuse me if it were theater, but it isn't.

Once again we encounter no problems at the border, where columns of trucks, their engines purring, are waiting in line to cross over to Chechnya. With all this cargo to inspect, the border

---

* A brand of Russian car manufactured by Lada.

guards are too preoccupied to pay much attention to private cars.

On the Rostov-Baku highway, we meet ramshackle carts, cars without license plates, trucks with improvised signs on their windshields declaring them to be "empty," and countless tanker-trucks hauling inflammable cargo. All the vehicles but the carts are hurtling along at a great speed. Lawlessness is the rule, on the highways no less than in society at large.

Through the dust, I can make out sentry boxes made of wooden boards with cardboard roofs. Old women have set up their paltry wares along the roadside—mountains of dry biscuits and canned tomatoes. Smoke escapes in dark curls from the houses set back from the road. To our left, there's a brown field of withered corn. In the far distance loom the familiar shapes of the mountains. Islam turns his head to tell me that Stinger* missiles cost $100,000 apiece, and that they enter Chechnya by way of Georgia.

Islam has an olive complexion and when he isn't sad, there's often a malicious glint in his eye. As far as I can tell, he always wears three days' growth of beard. I like him.

The air is quivering with the sound of mortar fire from the Federals. We have to swerve to miss a grain harvester; neither driver wants to brake. Swarms of black birds are circling over the highway. As we pass through the villages and small towns, we encounter familiar images: trucks piled high with sacks of sugar, tea, and flour;† quarters of beef suspended from the yawning trunks of cars; a Chechen flag planted by the side of the road; and,

---

* An American ground-to-air missile, fired from the shoulder.
† Coming from Krasnodar, to the south of Russia.

always and everywhere, caved-in gangrenous buildings pock-marked by shell bursts.

We are not driving unaccompanied; behind us, other racing aces are playing at Indy 500. These are fighters from Islam's band, and they're armed to the teeth. I glance behind and can see a driver clearly, his mouth deformed by the wad of gum he is chewing. He wears a camouflage cap, a T-shirt, and a khaki vest. His chest is studded with weapons and ammunition—a knife, a pistol, grenades—and he wears small black rectangular glasses: A miniature Rambo. This tough pose may be an affectation, but it's not entirely ineffective.

⌒

Here we are at last in "the city," as the Chechens call it: Grozny, their capital. Here every parcel of land shows traces of wars past, present, and future. Wild dogs roam the streets, barking. We park in front of the mayor's office, a concrete fortress, where Lechi Dudayev is still lord and master. My accompanying *boyviki* listen to Russian music with their eyes half closed. Islam has gone to find Fatima, a local journalist who will take me to meet Aslan Maskhadov. She emerges from the cube of concrete and steps into our car.

We head for Maskhadov's presidential palace, the former head-quarters of Grozneft, the state gas company, which was rebuilt after the earlier conflict. The flag of independent Chechnya is floating over a roofline bristling with antennae and satellite dishes.

Excitement pervades the crowd in front of the residence. All the men are armed, but they're laughing loudly and congratulating each other warmly; they do this by wrapping their arms around each other's waist or shoulders in the Caucasian manner. We park in front of a freshly repainted puppet theatre. "It's functioning," Islam tells me proudly. Fatima asks my two companions to remove the license plates from the car. As though by magic, two black curtains unroll to cover the car's rear windows. As far as the outside world is concerned, I don't exist. "This morning they fired on reporters from German television," Fatima explains. Those who did it have already been arrested and are being held at Bassayev's headquarters.

There's a thick traffic jam in the square in front of the Residence. It seems that Maskhadov is not at home, so Fatima suggests that we go to see Shamil Bassayev instead.

We untangle ourselves from the general confusion and set off for another part of town. Shamil's house is an imposing red brick structure with a large, shiny black gate. Facing it is another barricaded house, the home of Alla Dudayeva, widow of Dzhokhar Dudayev. On both sides of the street there are fruit trees protected by low brick enclosures. Another Niva passes, covered in a camouflage of mud. There are no cars in front of Bassayev's. Fatima goes inside to see what's up; several minutes later she emerges and gestures to us to come in. Shamil is at home and has agreed to see us.

The black gate closes quietly behind us as we drive in. An old armored Mercedes is parked in the courtyard. In the background, two women busy themselves over a fire, no doubt preparing lunch. A small bearskin rug is drying in the sun. Although the Russian television news has been reporting that this "Terrorist

Number One," the target of the Kremlin's Operation Antiterrorist, is surrounded, we find the Chechen commander enjoying a
quiet afternoon at home. Bassayev comes out, greets us with a
smile, and signals that stools should be brought to the middle of
the courtyard for us. He himself sits bolt upright in his chair with
his legs spread apart. He wears a khaki uniform and a black
ex–Soviet army belt. His green beret is decorated with a she-wolf,
the symbol of Ichkeria. The laces of his short black boots are
untied. He wears an enormous gold signet ring on the little finger
of his right hand. Ten or twelve members of his personal guard
stand around, hanging on his every word.

Bassayev is entirely at ease with western-style interviewing and
turns out to be a master of spin control. He studiously avoids
answering questions he doesn't like and generally chooses his
words with an eye to presenting the Russians in the worst possible
light. He seems optimistic and very, very sure of himself.

"How is this war different from the preceding one?" I ask for
openers.

"Now," he answers, "the Russians have dropped their masks.
According to our intelligence, they have been preparing to invade
Naursky [in northern Chechnya] since March 1998. In May, at the
frontier post at Kizliar [Dagestan], they even killed one of our
men as they tried to force their way through. We have known for
a long time that Russia wants not only to take revenge against us,
but also to solve various internal problems at the same time. What
kind of Russian state are we talking about? When every prime
minister in succession—Stepashin, Primakov, Putin—comes out of
the FSB, we're talking about a police state, pure and simple. And

Chechnya isn't their only target. When they've finished with us, they'll do the same in Georgia and Azerbaizhan. Russia will never give up her imperial ambitions. As for her war strategy, hardly anything has changed. The Russian troops are advancing by the same routes as before, and we are fairly certain that, if we put a mine in a certain place, a Russian soldier will step on it. On the other hand, they have become a tad more intelligent, for one reason and one reason only: Fear. They are so beside themselves with fear that they won't even advance over flat terrain. They can't bear heavy troop losses. They know that, if this happens, the Russian people will eventually rise up against this war."

Several seconds of silence follow. Everyone is respectfully absorbing the words of the Master.

"Are you surprised that the operation is labeled 'antiterrorist?'"

Bassayev throws his head back and laughs loudly, though the mirth seems forced. The men around him do exactly the same. Bassayev's open mouth reveals numerous missing teeth; his chestnut-colored eyes narrow to slits.

"If you're going to mount an antiterrorist operation, the first thing you need are terrorists!" he says. "The Russians are supposed to be putting a stop to Chechen terrorism, but they themselves are the real terrorists. They're terrorists on an international scale. They accuse us of fomenting terrorism in Dagestan, of having attacked our neighbors, but the war in Dagestan is really a war of national liberation. Russia has used it as a pretext for bringing more territory under her control. I can't repeat it often enough: The Russians will never give up their imperialist ambitions. In 1996, I was happy to throw those pigs out of the country, and I was hoping that we could close our doors before they could get back in. Unfortunately, we didn't close our doors firmly enough. But it's not a problem. We'll get them out."

Sidelong glances and nervous laughter all around.

"The Russians assert that there is no front line," I begin.

Bassayev interrupts cautiously: "For us, there is no front, properly speaking, either. There's only a Russian cat-and-mouse game in which we try to respond in a localized way. Six days ago, our men crossed the Terek River to take back five villages in the northern zone. And the Russians threw everything they had at us. They used everything short of the atom bomb. But we're not really worried about that: It would be to their disadvantage, because of the radioactive fallout."

Bassayev breaks out laughing once again. "In any case, it's in their interest to make it seem as if there's no front, so that the international community believes we have no government, that we're just a handful of terrorists. But let them carry on firing on us —time is on our side!"

My attempt to persuade him to talk about his relations with other figures in the Chechen independence movement fails miserably. "What do you reply to those who say that the Chechen command is not unified and that Maskhadov is powerless?" I ask.

"And do you know what the whole world says about Russia?" he answers, tit for tat. "That Yeltsin is a good-for-nothing, a pig pickled in alcohol, scarcely able to hold on to the Kremlin, that Russia is run by his family, and the whole place is going to hell. Which is true. In other words, I don't give a damn what the Russians say. We Chechens can steal from each other and tear each other's guts out, but we've always been united against the Russians, and today is no exception, *inch Allah*! They put out the same nonsense during the first war: Dudayev had no control; his army consisted of no more than 500 men; in two hours they could take Grozny; and the rest of the country in three! But if Maskhadov really had no power, the Russians would never have had any reason to invade Chechnya, because we would have been under their control already! They're putting out stories they know to be false in order to cover up the true state of affairs. They claim to have me surrounded by 150 men! Imagine that, when the Russian police, who don't even know their own laws, are capable of only two things: Breaking skulls with their clubs and extorting bribes."

He's on a roll. There's no way to interrupt him on this subject. On the Russians' plan to take Grozny, he responds with the same fervor: "They can have all the plans in the world. Wanting something doesn't necessarily make it so. As if we're just going to lie down and let them walk in.... They impose a cordon sanitaire around us, and we're supposed to sit down and drink tea with them? The quarantine should be around Moscow instead, because the Russian mafia constitutes a real menace to world order. As for Aslan Maskhadov, he was right to demand talks. We agree with that request, though we know that it will never be met. The Russians will never agree to talks as long as they aren't in [the Russians'] interest. And nothing will satisfy the Russians unless they are able to carry out their imperialist designs. Maskhadov is a clever tactician; by insisting on negotiations, he has succeeded in demonstrating to the West that the Russians don't want talks or stability in this region. They want one thing and one thing only: Chechnya without the Chechens."

Bassayev is pleased with himself; he has put his best face forward. He is completely unmoved by his reputation as "Terrorist Number One." Convinced of the justice of his actions, he is also indifferent to complaints made against him by the Chechen public. He tries to be faithful to his own myth, but, at the end of the day, just what does motivate him? That is the question that all the Chechens ask themselves. Most of them are convinced that Bassayev's chief preoccupation is himself.

The squeaking of the gate interrupts us. Khattab, Bassayev's right-hand man, walks in. Would it be possible to ask him a few questions as well, I ask. "He's very timid," Bassayev jokes, "but I'll go see."

Khattab agrees to talk with me, but inside the house, where he has already installed himself on a sofa. I take my shoes off. So that I can record our conversation, I go to join him on the sofa; but he stops me in my tracks.

"Women—over there," he mutters in an approximate Russian, pointing to the rug in front of him.

I do as I'm told.

Khattab sits up very straight on the sofa. He is wearing a camouflage uniform, a black belt, black boots, and a black beret, from which his long black hair escapes. A black beard covers his smooth face. No one really knows who he is or just what role he plays in the Chechen high command and the war against the Russians. He must be around forty, a veteran of the war in Afghanistan, a Jordanian, possibly, or a Saudi. He is constantly fingering a rolled-up map—"Chechen Positions on the Front"—which he refuses to let me see.

Before taking questions, Khattab bows his head and murmurs a few Arabic phrases to himself, no doubt some verses from the Koran. Then he's off. His Russian, though clumsy, is perfectly comprehensible, but his lecture is often repetitive in its denunciation of the "Russian imperialist enemy."

"Why wouldn't I have the right to fight on Chechen territory?" asks the Mudjahid, as he likes to be called. "Muslims have to help each other. Russia has attacked Tadzhikistan and Afghanistan in the past. They're doing the same thing here. We're not touching anyone. It's the Russian army who's coming to kill us. We've got to defend our territory, our women and children," he says heatedly.

To hear Khattab's hackneyed anti-Russian litany, you would think the Chechen forces were composed of gentle lambs devoted only to the cause of Islam: "Our only goal is to be allowed to live according to our own laws, the laws of the *charia*," he argues. "As long as this is denied us, we'll continue to fight. Politics play no part in this. We're waging a war of religion."

He gives the same simplistic analysis when the subject turns to the two attacks—the first at the end of August 1999, the second at the beginning of September the same year—against the Dagestani villages I visited. Both Karamakhi and Chabanmakhi were reduced to rubble by the Russian planes that had come to the aid of the Dagestani authorities: "There were more than 1,000 children and some five hundred women in those two villages. The Russians could at least have created a corridor for their evacuation instead of blindly bombing them. Dagestanis and Chechens have common roots, a common history; they've even shared the same imam. Why did the Russian army get mixed up in this? They're incapable of resolving anything by dialogue; they always have to send in troops. Here, in Chechnya, it's the same old story. They won't leave us in peace, let us live as we want."

During one of his numerous incursions in Karamakhi, Khattab married a Dagestani native. He is suspected of having participated in several assassination attempts during his "Chechen years," notably the December 1996 murder of six members of the International Red Cross, who were savagely strangled in their sleep at Novye Atagi. Khattab, however, prefers to pass for a victim himself. "We're tired of being surrounded by the Russians and fed up with their terrorist tactics," he says. "Now we're going to respond to arms with arms, to blood with blood. People here are terrified at the prospect of another war. All they want is to live in peace. But there's only one kind of peace, our own kind, the peace of Islam. We want no Russian peace."

On the subject of the Wahhabis, Muslim fundamentalists, Khattab prefers to say little. When asked how many Wahhabis he thinks there might be in Chechnya, he responds laconically: "Wahhabi, non-Wahhabi, it's all the same thing. Here there are only the Muslim faithful. We don't make any distinctions."

The stump of his right arm (wrapped in a black wool mitten) loses hold of the map, which falls to the floor. He scoops the map up quickly and adds in conclusion, "It was the Russians who invented that name. Ten years ago it didn't exist. We began to hear talk of Wahhabis only after the start of that war."

We are travelling on a country road that snakes its way through fields. A woman in a headscarf sits on the grass in the middle of a flock of sheep. An old man passes by on a cart piled high with hay. Neither he nor his horse seems to be disturbed by the rhythmic metallic rumblings whose volume is amplified by the echo from the surrounding mountains. We hear a series of loud explosions, then silence. The birds resume their singing. Then the salvos begin again.

At the side of the road, a rusted sign indicates our entrance into "Bamut, Immortal Fortress." The sign was put there after the first Russo-Chechen War in memory of the eighteen months during which combatants from this Chechen town resisted the Russian troops. Today Bamut, a stone's throw from the Ingushetia border, is a ghost town, abandoned five years ago when its inhabitants fled. With the renewed Russian attack on the Chechen republic, this ancient town, once home to eight hundred people, has again become a target for the Federals.

Since the start of Operation Antiterrorist, the Russian artillery has shelled this area every night. Missiles and rockets have dug countless craters in the fields. On the Chechen side of the border, some two hundred defenders under the command of thirty-year-old Khamzat, a former sergeant in the Russian army, camp out night and day. Their job is to prevent the Federals from crossing the border. The Chechens claim to have killed twenty-seven Russians and captured an armored carrier one night recently. "But as long as they keep to their positions, we don't react," Khamzat explains. "They're constantly provoking us. They're just waiting to begin an all-out offensive against us." He stands, arms crossed, weighted down with the armory of the *spetsnaz*:* An AK-47, ammunition, grenades of different calibers, and a long switch-blade knife.

The *boyviki*, all between the ages of eighteen and thirty, have been put up in the courtyard of an abandoned farmhouse, where they also store most of their light arms: Automatic pistols, grenades, grenade-launchers, and antiaircraft defense missiles. They are resting here after their tour of duty at the front, and they offer me tea. A litter of kittens comes running in. Sultan is polishing his rifle. "While I wait for my tour, I clean our weapons," he explains.

It's five o'clock, time for the changing of the border patrol. Ten men appear, each with a pair of binoculars. The men look tired. Ten others set off right away to replace them. It's not far to the edge of the forest, where the Federals are camped. The young Chechens march along at a good clip. When they arrive at the edge of the forest, they rapidly disperse, each going to his position. Three huts have been set up in the trees as improvised look-outs and there are five "bunkers" camouflaged with earth. The Russian camp—a line of white tents—is scarcely five hundred meters away. Through binoculars we can see the movements of the Russians' armored vehicles. The enemy forces will observe each other for hours.

---

* Russian special commandos.

"Instead of firing directly at our bases, as they claim they do, they fire off to the side at random targets," Sultan explains. "At Assinovskii, the neighboring village, where our wives and children are staying, they even landed an enormous ground-to-ground missile right on the cemetery. Bad luck for them: It was a Russian Orthodox cemetery!"

We pass by the spot on our way out of town. The missile is, in fact, stuck in the earth amidst the graves. The air smells pleasantly of pine resin.

At the frontier, in a sunken lane, a hooded silhouette approaches our car. It's an Ingush border guard. He signals to us to halt. Trenches have been dug to prevent vehicles from crossing. The man, who turns out to be more accommodating than he first appears, indicates a path around the obstacle.

We pass on.

Chapter 3

SLEPTSOVSKII is rife with rumors about the closing of the border; it's the subject of every conversation. Families are split up, some of them still in the "interior" and others already "outside," in Ingushetia.

"My father and my brother stayed behind in Grozny," Zima, visibly distraught, tells me on the plane from Moscow to Ingushetia. After a brief trip home, I'm on my way back to the war zone. "My husband was commuting constantly from Malgobek [an Ingush village] to Grozny to bring them supplies. But ever since yesterday he's been stuck on the Ingushetia side of the frontier, which has been closed. That's why I'm coming back from Moscow, where I've been staying for a few days with my cousin, to get a sense of the situation. Now I hope to cross over to Grozny and convince my father and brother to come back with me. Up until now they've refused to leave Chechnya. They thought this time there wouldn't be any war. Here, in Ingushetia, we're living fifteen or twenty to a room. But nobody pays attention to that. The important thing is to have heat and a roof over your head."

　　　　　　　　　　　　　▲

The main intersection of the small town of Sleptsovskii is in a perpetual state of chaos. The road leading east toward the Chechen border is closed; a Russian armored car blocks the route. Three soldiers repeat the same thing to the hundreds of refugees, who have come out of nowhere and are now milling around them: "No, it's closed, no one is allowed through." Or "No idea, no one knows when the corridor will be reopened. We're waiting for orders."

　　Sleptsovskii, which had only 5,000 inhabitants at the beginning of Operation Antiterrorist, has become a refugee center; it now holds tens of thousands. Women are selling soda, cigarettes, and bread from small stands along the road. Men in *papakha** are doing business in dollars. Toyka Musayev, an ex-director of the Grozny Telegraph Company and member of the now-defunct Chechen-Ingush Parliament, harangues the crowd from the midst of a large group of women: "We've decided to take up a collection," she announces. "We've had enough of standing around, doing nothing. As soon as I've collected enough money, we're going to buy white fabric and write slogans on it. And, tomorrow morning, at eight o'clock, we're going to plant ourselves right

---

* Fur hats.

across from the border. It's the only thing we can think of to attract the attention of the authorities. We are peaceful women whose only desire is to go back to our homes to take care of our families. Since the missile strike on Grozny, everyone wants to flee. It's the Russians who are the terrorists, not us! We have nothing to do with Bassayev and Khattab. We certainly didn't want to go to Dagestan. We don't want to have anything to do with this war. We're educated people!" she shouts.

As the Chechen refugees* pour into Ingushetia, the population of the small republic is growing dangerously. To meet what the Russian government still refuses to acknowledge as a "humanitarian catastrophe," the Russian Ministry for Emergencies (MtchS) has set up seven camps on Ingush territory. These camps, however, can accommodate only 17,000 of the estimated 170,000 refugees. In the Ingush capital, Nazran, only a few international organizations are represented: The outstanding French group, Médecins du Monde, the only one present in Chechnya, and the International Committee of the Red Cross.

"Of course, we must step up the pace of our food distribution," Zarema Kurkieva, the local director of the Red Cross, complains. "Since the beginning of September, we have received eighty tons of food and clothing, but that's only enough to meet the needs of 15,000 people."

She is waiting on the airport tarmac for the arrival of the

---

* Of the estimated 200,000 people who fled Chechnya in the fall of 1999, about 170,000 went to Ingushetia. Although the influx has strained Ingushetia's meager resources, Ingush President Ruslan Aushev sharply criticized Russia for not letting more people cross.

Finnish foreign minister. It is Finland's turn to fill the presidency of the European Union.

"We're hoping that she isn't coming just to look, without doing anything," Zarema explains. "This is our last hope for aid from abroad."

The minister Tarja Halonen,* will spend only five hours in Ingushetia and will visit two camps. For her, dialogue with the refugees is not easy. "I represent the European Union, I've come to help you," she repeats at every opportunity.

"Please, please, stop the war! Tell them to stop bombing us, to stop killing our children," the miserable Chechen mothers reply. The mothers and their children surround the minister.

"When the next mission comes, next week, you will have to explain your situation clearly," Halonen advises, in a professorial tone. Sometimes she asks questions; for instance, she turns to a woman seated on an improvised bed in a railway car, her arm around her sleeping child. "What kind of problems do you have?" she asks.

"We have no faith in either Yeltsin or Putin," the woman answers.

The minister draws a blank. She asks another question: "Does your child cry during the air raids?"

Answer: "We want a political resolution, not war."

The minister, at a loss for a response, offers the woman a clementine and moves on.

Outside, men stand idle; they have nothing to do. Children

---

* Tarja Halonen was elected president of Finland in March 2000.

play chase between the tents. Crowded buses wait. Cows graze. Babies cry. Gray smoke rises from a few of the tents. Two big fellows in the dark blue uniforms of the Russian Ministry for Emergencies are assailed with questions by the refugees, who sometimes take them to task simply for being Russian. Vladimir Khomukha, finally loses his patience: "What can I tell you? I'm working with you, for you, you can see that! Unfortunately, there's nothing I can personally do to reopen the frontier."

Although the men from the Russian Ministry for Emergencies do their best to be kind to the refugees, they cannot answer all the nagging questions put to them and they stand helpless. The United Nations High Commission for Refugees (HCR) has sent convoys of aid to the area, but has no intention of installing permanent camps in Ingushetia. "How can we allow more humanitarian relief from abroad while, officially, we are supposed to be treating this problem in the Caucasus as an internal Russian matter?" Vladimir grumbles. "Furthermore, the army runs its own affairs, and so do we. All this is supposed to be temporary. What can we do about it?"

That is the problem, and the president of Ingushetia, Ruslan Aushev, has admitted as much to the press: "Every day I receive offers of aid from abroad, but I cannot accept them. The official position is that all aid, financial or material, must pass through Moscow." According to the office of the president, the number of refugees could reach 280,000 if the frontier were reopened. "Moscow and I have differing opinions on this subject. High-level bureaucrats in Moscow persist in proclaiming that nothing unusual is going on in Ingushetia. I'd like to see them in the sights of the Russian bombers," Aushev mutters darkly. "If, in two weeks, Russia saw her population of 150 million go up by some 80 million, what would they call that, if not a 'humanitarian disaster?'"

The influx of civilian victims of the Russian offensive has filled the five hospitals of the Republic of Ingushetia. In the village of Suzhennskaya, some ten kilometers from the Chechen frontier, the trauma center is completely overrun. There are two children in each of its forty beds. In the corridors, the air is stifling. The halls are crowded with gurneys and metal beds. Visitors mingle casually and unhygienically with the patients. In Room 7, two women in headscarves are seated on either side of a bed. They are overwhelmed by the tragedy that struck their sons, two youths of fourteen and eleven, six days previously. One of the mothers, Leyla Magomadov, rises suddenly and begins, in short phrases interrupted by sobs, to tell her story: "My son, Iussup, and his neighbor, Umar, went out to play in the main street of our village, Novo Charoy. They had scarcely left when I heard the sound of Russian artillery close by. I began to scream. In the road, a hundred meters from my door, a scene of utter horror: Arms and legs, body parts, everywhere.... I saw my boy covered in blood, both his legs torn off by the impact."

Iussup listens to his mother, his big gray eyes turned to the wall. His skinny little trunk ends in two stumps. His legs were amputated the day before yesterday at the Chechen hospital in

Urus-Martan. Suddenly he turns to his mother and asks in a small voice, "Can I still go to school?" She answers that she has no idea.

"We could no doubt have saved his legs, if only the border had been open," Umar Mairsultanov, a Chechen doctor, explains sadly. "Gangrene set in during the delay, and we had to think about the boy's life rather than about his legs."

At Urus-Martan, "the doctors cried more than I did," the mother says. Flies are buzzing around Iussup's stumps. No one bothers to swat them away.

In a nearby room, I find three men whose arms and legs are swathed in bloody bandages. All three have been gravely wounded by a ground-to-ground missile that hit the central market in Grozny ten days ago. "You see how they go after terrorists! Because that's what they call us—terrorists!" Akhmed, thirty-five years old, repeats over and over, grimacing with pain. "Do you remember when Yeltsin and Maskhadov were exchanging kisses?* Those days are long gone! Russia has lost her honor," he adds between gasps for breath.

In a corridor with peeling paint, Leyla lies on an air mattress. Last week, her entire left side was mangled by a bomb as she was preparing to cross the border with a column of refugees. "It came from out of nowhere. Almost everyone was killed," she murmurs.

Most of the patients have been operated on without anesthesia, and hardly any medications are available. The hospital serves more as a kind of lodging than a place of healing. It cannot even provide food. Umar Mayrsuhanov, the Chechen doctor, explains: "The

---

* At the signing of the peace accord, in May 1997.

less gravely injured are sent to Nazran, and we keep the others, those who really can't be moved. Most of them have been wounded by ground-to-ground missiles or artillery fire. In two weeks, I haven't seen one gunshot wound, which goes to show that, in this war, there is almost no direct contact with Russian troops."

He compares the Chechen hospitals with those in Ingushetia: "Conditions are just the same. There's nothing there or here. It's been ages since we've seen any medications, even the most basic, such as aspirin or penicillin."

In this situation, it's every man for himself. Because the pharmacies are empty, the patients' families have to buy drugs on the black market, and they also have to cook for their hospitalized relatives. To make room for new arrivals, the staff tries to move the surgical patients out as soon as possible.

Two Chechens, victims of snipers, lie unconscious in the resuscitation ward. One of them, a twenty-four-year-old, who has been shot in the head, has been in a coma for the last two weeks. "He has no chance of survival. We don't know what to do with him," says Rosa, a nurse, who, like most of the other hospital personnel, is a refugee from Chechnya.

The room is clean, but devoid of medical equipment. There are no machines to monitor the young man's vital signs. Beside him lies an old man, another victim of a sniper's bullet to the head. Three doctors in green gowns hover over him. The patient has just come from the operating room, and the doctors are testing his reflexes. "Stick out your tongue," they demand. On their uniforms, I can read in yellow letters: "Panrussian Center for Disaster Care." These are highly qualified specialists sent from Moscow by the Ministry of Health.

"There are twenty-three of us based here in a field hospital we've set up. Our main task is to care for the refugees," explains Oleg Zokhokhovich, a neurosurgeon. Strangely enough, this team of itinerant doctors—whose task it is to rush to disaster areas in Russia or abroad—has its own medicines and its own resuscitation unit, but it distributes no aid to local hospitals. "Chechnya also has two brigades of six Russian physicians each," Zokhokhovich adds. Naturally, these doctors are stationed in the "liberated" territories.

Ready as they are to accept any kind of assistance, the local doctors keep a certain distance from the Russians. "Everyone," Umar, the Chechen doctor, tells me, "is sure that the Russian specialists are here for one thing and one thing only: To set up an emergency military hospital in case of heavy Russian losses."

To pass "through the mirror," or to get into rebel-controlled Chechnya, is increasingly difficult. Islam and I are now rumbling along side roads in a four-wheel-drive vehicle, accompanied by two Ingush border guards. We're heading south through a leafy mountainous area when we stumble upon the village of Arshty nestled at the base of a rocky spur. Below us, a few kilometers down a winding road, I can make out the ruins of Bamut, in Chechen territory.

We stop at a farm that belongs to relatives of Islam. Zarima, one of the daughters, chases down a chicken and wrings its neck: our lunch. We drink hot tea. Meanwhile, long, noisy columns of Russians are rolling through Arshty. They are getting ready to reinforce their positions. Islam disappears to check out the situation. In a few minutes he's back, and he orders me to get into the car right away: "We're leaving," he says tersely. "Time to go, and fast!" The farm women look disappointed. "What about the chicken?" they seem to be thinking.

I hear the motor of another car outside, but the bright violet-tinged rays of the sun make it difficult for me to see. "Get in the back," Islam tells me, "and crouch well down in the middle, between the two front seats." Eight other men crowd in around me in this small space. No one can move. The passengers speak for a moment in Chechen, then all fall silent. The car starts down the slope. My gaze is level with the gearshift. When we reach the bottom of the curve, the driver shifts into first and we start to climb again. Speed is of the essence. At the top of the incline, conversation starts again. Suddenly, with a squeal of tires, we stop. We get out. We are in Bamut, in a farmyard. The trip from Arshty took twenty-five seconds tops. Apparently, the men had crowded around me to screen me with their bodies from Russian snipers. We passed straight through the Russian positions, but they did not have time to react. "In any case, the ditch-diggers are conscripts. They haven't received any orders. There wasn't much danger," Islam says.

I am safe in the farmyard, surrounded by smiling *boyviki*, but my hands are trembling. An enormous clap of thunder from nearby: Russian guns. For the first time, I am in the thick of war in Chechnya, and there is no turning back. Artillery sounds on all sides, as though God were shaking sheets of corrugated iron above our heads; but my ears soon grow accustomed to the unusual noise. I light a cigarette. I must learn to live with this war, to feel at home with it, to master my reactions.

⌒

When I join them inside the abandoned farmhouse, the Chechen fighters are warming their feet at the stove. Assia is the only woman in the group. She has a sarcastic manner and dresses in a scruffy headscarf and mud-caked boots. She acts as an unofficial chief housekeeper for the band, feeding wood to the stove, watching the pots, doing the cooking and the washing up. Her specialty is *lavasch*, a flat, round, crusty type of bread. On this beautiful sunny afternoon, thirty or so hungry young men are gathered around a rectangular table, noisily slurping tea before they leave for the front. After tea, a shoe brush is passed from hand to hand; the soldiers must polish their shoes before they leave. "If you're going to die, you should look impeccable," Ruslan explains. "You must be ready to die at all times. So you've got to be washed and have your shoes shined."

A cry rings out: "Plane! Plane!" Quickly and precisely, everyone assumes his fallback position. The cars are pushed into a hangar, and we all rush to the other side of the building, which has been fitted out as a shelter. The Russian plane, which was barely audible until it arrived directly over us, is flying against the sun. We can see it only at the very last moment as it approaches the farm. An enormous droning black shadow fills the sky. Seconds after we spot the plane, bombs begin to fall, two at a time. A deafening noise shatters the tense silence. I notice that the physical appearance of the enemy seems to have drugged some of the men and depressed others. They're strangely quiet, waiting for the bombs to stop. Each man seems suddenly alone with himself and his mortality.

I join Assia in the "cellar," if it can be called that; it's really a stable set up as a dormitory. The flimsy wood walls offer little protection. Five or six soldiers are at our side, bent over their ammunition belts or tensed in a waiting position. The candle flame jumps each time a bomb hits. The strikes are close. I pace back and forth. My mouth is dry. All we can do is to wait.

"It's your first attack?" Assia asks, smiling, quite unperturbed.

"Yes," I reply.

"Don't worry, it'll be over soon," she tries to reassure me.

A young man offers me chewing gum. Another strums a guitar and begins to sing. They seem almost happy.

In the other room, which looks out onto the courtyard, ammunition is being passed rapidly from hand to hand to supply those who are firing outside. Pairs of shoes are lined up in a row next to the wall. A dozen young men are praying with their foreheads to the ground, facing Mecca.

The five *puliemiochiki*—machine gunners—are on their feet, their faces scanning the sky. Five others, including Islam, are helping them to target the plane, which is making a wide circle before coming back to drop another load of bombs on us. Everything happens quickly. The machine gun, which the Chechens call

"Beauty," is aimed straight at the enemy target. The steady rhythm of firing punctuates the air. Bamut has no antiaircraft defense system; no American Stinger missiles, either. "Too expensive," Khamzat, the commander of the two-hundred-man rebel force, explains. "For now we're getting along without them. As for the future, I can't forecast with any certainty. No one knows what might happen. The Russians don't dare to come up to our positions. We have almost no direct contact with them. It's only the artillery fire and the air attacks that are hard to reply to."

Each time the airplane passes overhead and each time a bomb explodes, the troops shout "Allah Akhbar!"* A shell has fallen so close to our hiding place that a fragment has rebounded into the courtyard. One of the men picks it up and tosses it to another, who quickly passes it off to a third as if it were a hot potato. No one can hold the scorching fragment for more than a few seconds. It remains hot for more than twenty minutes. At last, the plane disappears and we return to more normal occupations.

Assia crosses the courtyard to the kitchen, where the youngest soldiers help her with the dishes. "Do you think they'd take us in the French Foreign Legion?" one of them asks me seriously. Others put their shoes back on after their prayers. A third group prepares to assess the damage.

The bombs have exploded without hurting us—a miracle, it seems—but now for the reality of casualties, bomb craters, and burning metal; indeed, a wounded man has already arrived, and he must be taken right away to Urus-Martan to be examined by a

---

* Allah is great!"

doctor. Khamzat laces up his shoes and puts away his walkie-talkie. The weapons are quickly stacked in a corner where they will wait for the next alert.

Passing through the kitchen, the commander tucks a book under his arm that he's found lying by the stove, a collection of poetry by the Russian Romantic poet Mikhail Lermontov.

"If the Russians think that we have any intention of letting their bombs rain down on us and doing nothing about it, they're making a serious mistake," he says. "We have a completely different plan. We're almost certainly going to regroup soon in Grozny, where we'll be placed under the command of the chief of the southwest regions. But until he sends for us, we'll stay put and confront the enemy, at our own peril."

⌂

The sky is once again a vast stretch of peaceful blue. We'll take advantage of the weather and leave for Grozny while it's still daylight. Akhmed, a friend of Islam's, is driving us in a red Nissan Patrol. The rear windows have been replaced by cardboard. The shattered windshield threatens to implode at any moment into a thousand pieces. We dare not take the road, a target of incessant artillery fire; instead, we cross the fields and ford rivers. The sun, while low on the horizon, is still brilliant and could mask the sudden arrival of a bomber. I'm always glancing behind us at that treacherous star. If a plane appeared, what would we do?

Akhmed, who is worried about the fog forming on our kaleidoscope of a windshield, stops suddenly in the middle of a flat field within firing range of the Russians; he searches about for a bit of rag so that he can wipe the windshield.

"Are you crazy or what?" Islam yells.

"I can't see a thing," Akhmed complains.

We laugh, though a bit nervously, as we continue on our bumpy path. Later we come to a paved road. It's dusk. There are few people about and almost no traffic. We have to crawl along because of our shattered windshield. As we pass through one village after another, our headlights pick out the frightened faces of the inhabitants—men, women, and children. Groups of men are standing about talking; others are waiting for buses that may never come. A few old women wrapped up in woollen hoods are dragging metal shopping carts behind them. Armed men, the kind we met at the front, are nowhere to be seen.

We arrive in Grozny in the evening and head straight for old Daud's to find a bed. We hammer on his door, but no one answers; either he can't hear us or else he's afraid to open up. Or he might be dead, Akhmed adds. We give up here, but we must find shelter of some kind for the night. Islam suddenly remembers the house of some acquaintances of his who left Grozny ten days ago; and so we sleep in their dank, dark abandoned building, huddled up tightly next to each other to keep warm.

The market in the center of Grozny is in ruins, but it continues to do business. The ground is littered with the debris caused by the ground-to-ground missile that landed here thirteen days ago.

Ironically, the arms market, a hundred meters away, wasn't touched by the impact.

Most residents of the town center have left to seek refuge in Ingushetia or Dagestan or in the outlying villages. We rarely see women and children in the streets. The only people we meet are *boyviki* with Kalachnikovs in their hands and strings of grenades across their chests; they come to the market to buy little fresh rolls. Even though prices are now ten times higher than they were at the beginning of the war, bread still costs only a few cents. The morning is calm, the sky azure. When the nearby guns of the Russian artillery are still, there is almost total silence. In Grozny, there are no more dogs; even the strays have disappeared. There is no birdsong. After five o'clock, when night falls, the city is dead. Except for the handful of houses lit with electricity from a generator, the town is completely dark. No gas or water either. The few residents of the capital who have chosen to stay live like peasants, at the mercy of the natural rhythm of daylight and dark, warmth and cold. Their long nights last from five in the afternoon until seven in the morning, interrupted only by heavy thuds of artillery or salvos from Grad missiles.

Madina Lobsskaya, a young reporter for the only state television channel in Chechnya, is in her concrete studio; the television camera sits on the floor because there is no furniture. She lets her anger show: "When I think that Putin recently said that there's no one left in Grozny but combatants and prostitutes!" she says. "Where does he get that? What right does he have to talk about us that way? I personally have stayed here and continued to work so that the few people who own television sets can get information from the Chechen side!"

On a recent afternoon, Madina and her Chechen cameraman were the only reporters present when Russian planes attacked a column of refugees. The video images are horrifying. Two packed buses suffered direct hits. Dead bodies lie everywhere.

"The few Chechen journalists who work here for Russian television—the Russians don't dare send their own reporters here—didn't want anything to do with this footage. They told me that no Russian channel would air it."

I later learn that the Russian authorities announced that same day that they had attacked a column of "terrorists."

Next door to an abandoned circus, whose cupola is dotted with black bullet holes, stands a large white concrete building with a gleaming plaque: "City Hall of the City of Dzhokhar." On the front steps, a man is seated in an old chair between cast iron sculptures of the symbol of Chechnya: Two she-wolves, crouched respectfully on either side of their master. The man is Lechi Dudayev, the mayor; he pointedly refers to Grozny as "the City of Dzhokhar," which has been its official name since it was rechristened in 1997, on the eve of the presidential elections. This large, handsome young fellow, who has a shaved head, bright blue eyes, and a blond beard, is the nephew of Dzhokhar Dudayev, the Chechens' rebel-hero who died at the hands of the Russians in 1996. "Actually, I prefer to be addressed by my real title, Deputy Chief of the Armed Forces of the Republic and Commander in Chief of the City," Lechi Dudayev says with a crooked smile.

His conversation is constantly interrupted by harsh squawks from his walkie-talkie; he continually fiddles with the radio.

"The Russians are simply there where we allow them to be,

namely on the plain," he explains. "Our policy is to keep them from moving up to positions that we consider strategically important. All this is just a prelude to our victory. The Russians are subject to pressure from the West, whereas we can take all the time we want. That's one of the fundamental differences between us."

The artillery is firing more heavily. The rounds sound louder and more distinct. Dudayev doesn't pay the slightest attention though he does invite me inside. He set himself in front of a colored portrait of his uncle, which brightens the gray wall of his bunker, and continues his thought: "I like to compare the Russians to a child who is trying to control himself and not gobble up a cake that he knows he's allergic to. In the end, will he eat it or not? Will he make himself sick or not? Will they come to Grozny to get us or not? Look in the eyes of our soldiers. Those eyes are crystal clear. They're composed, serene. On our side, there's not a trace of panic."

The office of the mayor of Dzhokhargha* is getting colder and colder; but the commander hasn't finished yet: "The Russians have no sense of honor. They view everything that happens there, in Russia, like a movie. But they don't realize that all this is going to work to their disadvantage. They use their media and the local population to impress the rest of the world. Putin has built his entire career on Chechnya!"

But for the moment, Dudayev explains to me, the real war has not yet begun. "Chechen troops haven't yet engaged the Russian troops. The Russians have allowed themselves to fight only against

---

* "The city of Dzhokhar" in Chechen.

the civilian population and the Chechen refugees. They can call those military victories if they like, but that's simply ridiculous!"

It's such a beautiful day that Dudayev opens the French doors to the terrace. He smokes a cigarette in the sun. Meanwhile, I set up my satellite telephone so that he can call a friend in Holland.

"Are you married?" he asks me abruptly.

Without waiting for my answer, he adds, half joking and half serious, "What would you say to the idea of tying your fate to a man whose wife has abandoned him? Why don't you come and live here with me, in the country of the wolves? Look how well we live here."

His gaze roams over the panorama of ruins surrounding us.

Suddenly, his walkie-talkie begins to crackle without interruption. End of conversation. The mayor closes the curtains of his third-floor office and asks me to follow him downstairs.

"We may have an air attack soon," he says by way of explanation.

I wait: Nothing. Then I get back in the car.

Near the mayor's office, in a tumbledown red brick house that appears to be abandoned, lives Taissa Mikhailovna, a sixty-eight-year-old Russian, born in Chechnya. It's colder inside her house than it is outside.

"Here in Chechnya," she begins, offering me pickles from a jar of dirty water and apologizing because she has no forks, "I am among my own people. I was born here, and I'll die here. During the first war, I went into exile in North Ossetia. This time, I'm going to stay. My husband is dead, and I have no more reason to live.... My family's in Russia, but I don't consider them my family any longer. My real family is here; they're my neighbors."

This ex-nurse is the one who is hardest on her compatriots: "Putin: They should hang him! Yeltsin: They should ... I prefer not to finish my sentence."

Tears trickle down her cheeks. It's chiming six and it's dark outside; Taissa is getting ready to spend another sleepless night in her iron bed in an icy room with a rough cement floor.

⌒

Thankfully Daud has reappeared and we spend the night at his place in two rooms overheated by a wood stove. All night long, the old man tosses and turns and makes loud moaning noises in his sleep. All night long, he coughs as he cries, and cries as he coughs.

At 6:00 A.M., Islam offers to drive me to the other side of town for a wash. There has been no running water for a long time now; but I am curious, so I agree to go with him. We must make a strange sight, crossing the devastated city in our wreck of a car. Apart from a few *boyviki* with berets and ammunition belts, we encounter almost no one in the streets. We reach the outskirts of the city around Pervomayskoye. On the high ground, we can see the Russian positions; the aircraft set off from here all last night with their cargo of bombs. As I tried to sleep, I could hear the droning of the planes as they drew nearer, slowed, circled low, and dropped their deadly loads. "They let them go when the mood strikes," Islam murmured to me in the dark. "It makes no difference to them." I wasn't afraid, but there I was, wrapped like a mummy in my covers, forced to contemplate the end of my existence. I thought of all the others like me in Grozny that night, tossing in their beds, yearning for sleep, but listening instead to the throbbing of planes overhead and the heavy thud of enemy fire.

Islam leads me to a field of abandoned silos. It's 6:30 A.M. and the mauve sky is dotted with cottony clouds. The poetic beauty of the landscape seems oddly out of place. I can't shake off the night of war.

In the middle of the field, a hot spring emerges miraculously from the earth. The spring is surrounded by an almost perfect oval of stockade fencing. Behind a hastily improvised screen I can glimpse a hole in the ground. It's full of steaming, bubbling water. You let yourself down into the water by means of ladders attached to the hole's hot mud walls.

We're not the first ones here. Ruslan, the commander of one of the Grozny sectors, is in the midst of his bath. His companions try to keep warm while they wait patiently for their chief to finish his ablutions. They sit in their car with its motor running. Apparently the *boyviki* use this sulfurous spring for their clean-ups; the soldiers take turns bathing, and, if a woman comes, the tradition is for them to get out and give her fifteen minutes on her own before they return to the water. I choose to wait instead. There is almost total silence. Ruslan climbs out of the hot spring. I chat with him as he shaves himself in front of a piece of mirror. He is clean-shaven, but some of the *boyviki* wear beards. "Most of the bearded ones are Wahhabis," he explains. "But I am not."

Standing in the soft light of the rising sun, this former professor of geography expresses confusion about the renewed war. Although it doesn't surprise him, it seems to sadden him deeply:

"Of course, I was already in command of an *otriad** in the earlier war, but it wasn't at all like this. The Russians thought there would be a blitzkrieg, that it would all be over in seventy-two hours. That's why they rushed in and the encounter was very bloody. This time, they're holding back. We all notice it. The tension rises every day, but they never change their tactics: They sweep the area with air strikes and heavy artillery before advancing even a few meters. They've been bombarding Grozny from the outskirts for several weeks. Now what?"

I ask him how the Chechen rebel forces should respond.

"We have already begun another kind of war, a partisan war, and the Russians will have a lot of trouble defeating us," he replies. "They have some 90,000 troops surrounding us, divided into very hierarchical regiments. They use troops who never enlisted to come here. Meanwhile, we have 25,000 men in the city of Grozny alone. They're split up into mobile units, and they have all chosen to defend our country. That's the big difference!"

Ruslan dries his face and cleans his teeth with a bit of soap. He slips on his ammunition vest over his clothes, adds his grenades, his walkie-talkie, and, finally, his army cap. He puts the cap on backwards, like a rapper, then sits down on a bench to continue our talk. "Despite the 'advances' of the 'fearless' Russian army, I'm sure they won't get far. There are limits to their strategy. Ours, however, hasn't really begun to be put in place. And we have several options for our arsenal. We can suddenly turn up where they're least expecting us. We also have chemical weapons. For

---

* Russian word for a detachment of troops.

now we have no need to use them, but you never know. With all they're throwing at us, we might be driven to try something more deadly," he adds darkly.

The young green-eyed commander has difficulty in explaining his personal relationship with Russia. Because of his civilian career, he has mixed feelings: "I would like to remain loyal to Russia. I lived there and studied there, and my wife is Russian. But recent events have forced me to change sides. I do it for my children and the future of our country. I have two sons. The older one is two, the younger two months. He was born into this dirty war. My wife, Lyudmila, didn't want to leave Chechnya for Ingushetia. She decided to stay here. That's a good thing; she sets a fine example for the wives of my men. We need the support of our loved ones."

It's my turn for the bath. Islam waits until Ruslan's car has disappeared around a curve before allowing me to get undressed and slip into the water. The bubbling liquid is burning hot. I can feel the soft, sticky mud under the soles of my feet. Sitting in the water, I look up and contemplate the fine day that's dawning overhead. The air is rumbling, but I'm already used to it. Other than that, everything is calm. For the first time in days, I feel at peace. Because we're in a hurry, Islam violates the "law," undresses quickly, and slips into the swirling water beside me. He has found a cake of pink soap and rubs my head with it. I feel his strong hands on my scalp. For a moment we are outside of time, a hundred miles away from the war.

"Get out right now, get dressed quickly, and wait for me in the car," he says suddenly. I make my way up the ladder carefully, taking care not to slip in the mud. Inside the car Islam has put the heat on high. I wait for him.

On our way back, we note the damage caused by the bombs that have fallen during the night—new craters of freshly dug earth. I feel tired and clean. We pass through the center of town again, taking the curved tunnel with a foot of stagnant water in the bottom, and then the Minutka intersection. "Normal" life has resumed once more—little bread rolls are piled up on the stalls; women in headscarves are squatting to smooth out the plastic sheets on which they will display their sad little wares.

⌂

Around ten, we go to rebel "headquarters" in the hope of meeting President Aslan Maskhadov. He isn't there; Vice President Kazek Makachov is in command. He sits in our car so that we can talk "more peacefully." No need, he says, for me to seek Chechen accreditation; it will suffice that I am on the spot. We are parked in front of a ruined building; on the porch someone has written in Russian: "This building is under surveillance." Bodyguards are posted here and there in the street. Makachov, a small talkative man, seems busy and discouraged at the same time: "We have no more hospitals or maternity hospitals. The Russians have bombed them all. That's what they mean by terrorist bases! They have become so cynical that for them, terrorist and Chechen is the same thing. Putin tried to claim at the Helsinki summit that this was some kind of "special operation." But that's an out and out lie. There are specific means of combating terrorism. But nowhere in the world do you fight terrorism on the scale of a whole country, of a whole people!" he exclaims in revulsion. Then he explains to Islam how to find Maskhadov.

☖

It isn't easy to meet the president, who was elected by the Chechen people but disavowed by Moscow at the start of their Operation Antiterrorist. Aslan Maskhadov is not in hiding; he is simply protecting himself. Two Russian missiles have recently fallen on the central market in Grozny and on a maternity hospital opposite the president's residence. Since then, he has stopped working in his office.

"I dropped in there only yesterday," he notes with a wink, "but I decided not to give them that pleasure."

Instead, the Chechen president changes offices every day; there are plenty of vacancies to choose from because most of Grozny's inhabitants have fled.

Today, Maskhadov's office is a few minutes' car ride from the center, in a house with a grapevine climbing up its façade. In the courtyard, behind the high brick walls, seven bodyguards are standing about chatting. Others are reading *Versia* ("Version"), a Moscow weekly. Still others carry attaché cases in one hand and typed documents with the letterhead "Ichkeria" in the other. The purring of the electric generator obscures most noise. A tabby cat rubs herself against the legs of one of the guards. He bends down to take her in his arms, then lifts her to his shoulder; this game is clearly a habit of theirs. It's the hour of prayer. We wait patiently for the prayers to end and are admitted to the house by a young man dressed in a prayer cap and camouflage.

In a vast, ice-cold room, we find Aslan Maskhadov. His manner is calm and even playful. He is also dressed in khaki camouflage. A bulletproof vest under his jacket lends him an imposing breadth. His improvised "desk"—a small square table—is covered with a plastic Chechen flag, some file folders, and several student notebooks bearing the simple title in felt pen: Aslan Maskhadov. Maskhadov speaks slowly, choosing his words carefully. He inquires about my security precautions. He wants to know how I managed to reach Grozny and asks about the current situation at the Ingushetia border. He is surprised to encounter so few journalists, but he "understands," he says.*

He speaks in a low voice, as though he were sharing a confidence. "A war is going on here," he begins, "even if the Russian media pretend it doesn't exist and minimize the losses. The truth is that they're engaged in the total destruction of our population."

Maskhadov describes in detail the weapons employed by the Russians. He knows what he is talking about because he was an artillery specialist in the Russian army. Then he holds forth on the Russians' recent targets, the central bazaar, the maternity hospital, and Hospital Number 2: "When the Russians say that they target

---

* Russian authorities have virtually banned international and local journalists from reporting on the conflict in Chechnya, often by manipulating accreditation requirements. Journalists are required to hire armed security guards when working in Ingushetia. These guards have been instructed not to let journalists enter Chechnya. Many journalists have been arbitrarily arrested, questioned, detained, and deported by Russian officials in Chechnya.

terrorists only, I certainly hope that no one believes them. They even bombed Shamil Bassayev's house, though he sold it ages ago." He laughs bitterly.

According to Maskhadov, the Chechen forces have already succeeded in bringing down seven planes and ten helicopters, and they have destroyed at least two hundred pieces of Russian artillery. The president professes ignorance of the details of Russian strategy, but he insists on the determination of the Chechen fighters: "You see, here I am this morning, within reach of Russian rockets. No doubt, in some other country, that would create panic, but here, in our world, all is calm. I know all the Russian generals directing operations; they were already in place during the earlier war. I simply don't understand how they can carry out the same operations all over again. They know very well that we won't allow them to take our cities, that it will turn bloody. How can they not realize that they've got to bring this war to an end?"

Maskhadov has tried to stave off war many times over, notably by attempting to meet with his counterparts in the neighboring republics of the Caucasus and southern Russia. Before this second conflict began, he met with the presidents of North Ossetia and Ingushetia, but their attempts at cooperation have come to little. "The Russians simply will not allow us to organize. I had concrete proposals to put to our neighbors. In the first place, we need a combined security force. Five hundred from each country would make up an international peace force, which we would station on the frontiers with Russia. We would also combine forces in the fight against terrorism and banditry, so that we could do something about kidnapping in particular."

None of Maskhadov's plans worked out. Now the Chechen president hides his disappointment behind forced laughter.

He lists his own questions in a slightly annoyed tone: "What do the Russian leaders really want? How will they prove to the world that we're all a bunch of terrorists? Moreover, where are these terrorists? I'm looking for them myself! Our tragedy is that for four hundred years, they haven't been able to prove even one of the misdeeds they've accused us of, including even the most recent bombings in Moscow."*

Maskhadov springs up and begins to pace about the room, talking about himself in the third person: "What is the point of all these military operations? So that Maskhadov will get down on his knees before Russia? Don't the Russians realize that he's probably the only Chechen who has remained loyal to them? I am convinced that we could have come to an agreement with Russia, especially in our economic relations. I had already told President Yeltsin that I was ready to defend Russian interests in the Caucasus. I asked him why he constantly needed to make war against us, but he didn't answer me. Chechnya is a veritable citadel. They'll never take us!"

He pauses for a moment and sits down. He looks grave, almost worn out, but he continues: "Now, I can only repeat myself: Enough! We've had enough already! Even in the West, everybody has had enough of this Chechen business. If this continues, I will simply make the decision to put myself at the service of Western

---

* Maskhadov is referring to a series of apartment explosions that killed some three hundred people in Russia in September 1999.

interests in the Caucasus. I will represent the West here, and Russia will no longer have an ally in the region."

When I ask him what progress he has made in the country since his election, his answer is surprisingly honest: "Nothing, unfortunately. I have been able to reconstruct practically nothing. Everything has been destroyed. But I should add, for those who think that I have no control in Chechnya, that the only reason I haven't succeeded in reestablishing order here since 1997 is that I have been afraid of Russia. If I had tried to restore order among the various armed groups, we wouldn't have been able to avoid internal conflicts, and that would have resulted in a civil war. That's exactly what the Russians were waiting and hoping for so they could launch another offensive. I am proud that at least we have been able to avoid that, namely, civil war. When all is said and done, war with the Russians is better than war among the Chechens! And then, of course, I'm a military man, and an independent Chechnya needs a civilian president."

He sighs deeply. "But for now, with this war, I think that I'm still the man for the job."

⌂

Leaving the city, we drive past Hospital Number 2, an enormous brick building, which is still standing but in ruins; it is occupied only by crows and dry leaves dancing in the wind. Five days before, a bomb destroyed the northern façade of the building, which is now a pile of rubble. A water tap flows perpetually. All the doctors have disappeared. In front of the gates at the entrance are a series of kiosks labeled "Pharmacy," still stocked with medicines, which no one has had the thought, or the time, to steal.

☖

Day is dawning in Achkoy-Martan, where we stopped for the night. We're forty-five kilometers southwest of Grozny. All night long, artillery fire sounded, first on the right, then on the left of the house. Flares flashed, illuminating the sleeping house. Silence. Then explosions.

Magomed, the owner of the property, was born in Kazakhstan during the Chechen deportation. He returned here, to the land of his ancestors, as soon as he could. He is proud that his son, Dzhokhar, who is eleven, will one day become the eighth in a succession of landowners. The property will stay in the family, passing from generation to generation. This war makes him ill. "Come, I'll show you a little terrorist, born just a week ago," he says sarcastically. At the bottom of the farmyard, surrounded by chickens and turkeys, a dozen sheep are enclosed in a wooden stall. A lamb stands shakily between the forelegs of its mother: "There he is, the terrorist!" Magomed is pleased with his joke.

Magomed is a farmer; everyone around here is. But the real profession of this former sergeant, who served in Kiev, Ukraine, is construction: "In the Soviet era," he says, "we lived under Communism, and all things considered, it was much better. Back then, we could go where we wanted to. I don't know how many times I crossed the country, building houses. In those days, I had a good reputation. But when the Union was destroyed, I suddenly became an enemy of the people, like all the others of my generation. It happened from one day to the next."

Magomed is dark-skinned and has a black mustache. He speaks loudly, in a high-pitched voice, and sometimes has to search for his words in Russian. "I'm no intellectual, but I really don't understand this war. This Putin, what does he want? I am appalled to be labeled a terrorist in front of my children. I share everything I have with the others in the village. This morning, my daughter, Aza, gave our neighbor half the milk from our two cows. Is that being a terrorist?"

He sighs, then continues quickly, "Five of my six children are in the hospital. They were burned by bomb fragments a week ago. My wife is also in the hospital, but she has been there for a long time—four months already—because she has cancer. And they won't let me cross the frontier to see them! It's the Russians who are going to force us to take up arms! What would you do in my place?"

A week ago, five of Magomed's six children (who are between three and sixteen years old), were in the main street of the village, about a hundred meters from their house, when an air raid began. They were all injured in the explosion; sixteen-year-old Aza was at home at the time, helping her father.

"Suddenly, there was thick black smoke, and I saw my daughters running toward me. They were burned all over on their backs," Magomed continues.

He brought the wounded children to the burn unit of the hospital in Urus-Martan, twenty-five kilometers away. There, the doctors advised them to cross over into Ingushetia as quickly as possible, to the hospital at Sleptsovskii. Magomed is not even certain that they ever arrived. He has not been able to cross the border because Chechens are no longer allowed to leave the country.

"In any case, the Russians will lose this war," he declares, his voice rising. "No matter what happens! They're ready to use chemical weapons, because they think that we have them, too. But how could that be, when none of our factories is working?"

Aza, stick-thin legs poking out from under her short skirt—worn with her father's permission—has fine, dark features and laughing eyes. She is permanently consigned to the kitchen, and she stays in the background as father, the patriarch, speaks. Aza's long day is filled with countless household tasks. She sweeps the floors with her straw broom, prepares meals, washes the dishes, cleans the shoes of the new arrivals, tends to the candles, and tidies the house. Magomed fetches eggs from the hen house, feeds the animals, stokes the wood stove, and visits the neighbors to gather news. No one has a radio, and the electricity was cut off ages ago. The only news that reaches the village is filtered, brought by the occasional visitor.

Aza serves us tea at her father's command and brings the documents that Magomed wants to show me.

"In 1986," Magomed recalls, "I deposited 36,000 rubles [about $1,200] in a savings account. It was everything I had in the world. At the time, I thought of myself as a rich man. If I had known for one moment that we were going to have a first war in 1994, and then a second one today, I would never have put this money in a bank. I would have gathered up my family, sold my two cows, and left."

For where?

"For Kazakhstan, for example. Exile is better than war. Because, if this goes on, in two years my son, who's not going to school, won't just have a machine gun in his hands but maybe an atomic bomb."

Another early morning in Achkoy-Martan. If he hasn't slept well, Magomed doesn't let it show. In his kitchen, he offers us an omelet, made with canned tomatoes, and homemade bread. "I've gathered together our most precious and important possessions and put them under lock and key in that room. [He indicates a closed door.] And as long as I'm alive, no Russian will take anything away from here. This waiting that we're all doing is much worse than it is for condemned prisoners in their cells. They, at least, are fed and housed, and know that death will come. If the Russians come, I'll kill the first two or three, and then who knows?... This morning we're sitting around this table, talking and laughing, but from one minute to the next, everything can stop. Only Allah can help us!"

He has scarcely finished his sentence when an enormous thud breaks the silence. The sound rushes at us from the back of the house, shakes the kitchen windows, and reverberates in a nearby explosion. Everything in the house vibrates, including the walls. Miraculously, the windows remain intact.

"There, that's only a little distance away, in our street. There will certainly be wounded. That's what they call firing on the 'bases' of the combatants," Magomed murmurs, dismayed.

He has no appetite for his omelet. Instead, he pulls on his heavy boots, grabs his coat and hat, and hurries out into the street. We follow in his footsteps. Flames are already visible.

The Russian rocket has made a direct hit on a farm five houses away from us. It has destroyed everything in its path; a family of eight has perished. Riamzan, the gravedigger, has already arrived. A crowd has formed around the burning house. They have already extracted several bodies, including four children. The men look grave, the women wipe their eyes with the corners of their scarves; children have stopped playing to stare at the scene. No one says a word. The men go off to pray together for the victims. The women return home to see to the remains of their daily lives. In the distance, the guns thunder without a pause.

⌂

It is almost easier to get into war-torn Chechnya than it is to get out. Islam, Akhmed, and I have left our car "for safekeeping" and have come by taxi, then on foot, to the frontier village of Assinovskii, the last town before Ingushetia. It is around half past noon, and I am sitting in the sun on the front steps of Akhmed's former house, listening yet again to the sounds of war. One begins to distinguish among them; the ear tunes itself quickly. Children learn to go on playing under the sound of heavy reconnaissance aircraft passing overhead. According to Islam, they're not combat planes; their job is to register "the slightest movement of the bandits." Oddly enough, their buzzing sound reminds me of some of the most peaceful moments of my childhood, in Haute-Savoie in summer, when we used to watch the white trails from airplanes in the sky above our heads. But graceful bombers, with slender bellies and black predator wings, also emerge suddenly out of the sun's glare, the better to hide themselves. Artillery fire is unique; the Grad missiles fall with the sound of hail.

I am a perturbed by one important change: This time, in Assinovskii, the firing I hear is not aimed at us, but it is passing over our heads. For now we are at the source of the shelling, in a village already occupied by the Russians. They are firing on Bamut, the "impregnable fortress" of Khamzat.

The frontier post isn't far off, but I don't dare pass through it with my two companions because of my identity papers. The Russians wouldn't appreciate a western journalist's snubbing their perfectly choreographed official tours.

Akmed's house isn't ice-cold yet, as he was living there with his young wife until recently. Ten days ago, they decided to leave for Ingushetia because of the shelling. Akhmed's wife, Lena, eleven years his junior, is now waiting for him on the other side, in Sleptsovskii; Radima, Islam's wife, is waiting there as well. We are in some doubt about the best way to cross the border. Following official procedure is fraught with difficulties, but the only alternative is to wait until nightfall and to start walking—straight into the Russian positions. Islam and Akhmed know every blade of grass and clump of earth on this flat plain. This is where they played as children and went to war as adolescents.

We enter the living room, or what remains of it, by climbing in through the window. When they left, Akmed and Lena took their furniture away for safekeeping. With the exception of an immense double bed, which was too big to fit in the back of the truck, the house is bare. We are so exhausted that we fall asleep, all three of us, on the mattress, at about 4:30 in the afternoon. I sink into sleep as into a hot bath. My limbs feel like lead. Dreams fill my head. There's an airplane following me; but in my dream the town is modern and the plane fires laser beams as I run through the streets.

We wake in the black of night, and we've run out of candles.

When your familiar, domestic points of reference disappear, you quickly lose your sense of time. The next few minutes are all that matter; they're charged with weight and with intense emotion. In Chechnya I have to make a constant effort to remember which day of the week it is. Today must be Sunday, November 7, the Soviet national holiday.*

"This evening, things are really going to be popping. They'll drink like fish and shoot their guns off in every direction," my two guardian angels prophesy.

The night is black as soot, but full of stars. Around eight or nine o'clock, we set off on foot for the outskirts of the village, where the rows of houses stop and the fields begin.

"We'll need to walk a good twenty kilometers because of the detours," Islam whispers in my ear. "It's important not to make

---

* The anniversary of the revolution of October 1917 falls on November 7 because of the difference between the Georgian and the Julian calendars.

the slightest noise! You mustn't even sniffle or sneeze. At some point we may be passing less than twenty meters from the Russians."

I'm afraid, but I'm ready to march for hours through the cold and the mud. It's so dark that I can't see my hand in front of my face, but Islam is moving forward as if we were in daylight. He holds my hand tightly and steers me along. A great force emanates from his fingers. I have the impression that, if he raised his arm, I would fly into the air. I will do whatever he tells me.

I know that my life this evening is in Islam's hands. I know that I have no choice in the matter. I know also that he doesn't want to die; he wants to see his son grow up. That's what gives meaning to his life. He told me so himself, and that knowledge reassures me. They are killing his people, his friends, his family, and his country. Everything is destroyed, but still the Chechens stick together, clinging to one another, as tight as glue. Waiting for worse to come.

How troubled I am by this war! I am shifting constantly between two worlds and yet I want to plunge wholeheartedly into one of them—their world—the one that is the farthest from my own. That must be why I'm here. And that's why Islam frightens me with his talk of "the meaning of life." His life is so foreign to me, even though it has much more meaning. Each time he looks at me, even in the dark, he speaks to this yawning need in me, this emptiness I have inside.

We must turn back to Akhmed's house in Assinovskii. Flares are illuminating us every five seconds along the way. "Too risky," Islam says. "Especially with you!" It suits me fine; I am yearning for sleep. Tomorrow, I'll cross the border alone, in a bus, in the company of other women. The two young men will walk across the fields the following night.

Chapter 4

I T'S THURSDAY, November 25, 1999. Larissa and one of her six sisters, Lida, are tidying up the unsold stock in the small wooden kiosk their father built for them—Snickers bars, Russian candies, soda. They've grown used to the rumbling of Russian armored carriers, which grind past them along the long, straight road leading to the frontier with Chechnya, less than a kilometer away.

On this Thursday, an armored car stops in front of Larissa's kiosk, where the two sisters have already lighted their candles. (The area has no electric power.) Four soldiers get out; one of them opens fire directly on the kiosk. Larissa, inside, is hit in the right foot. With her sister's help, she tries to flee. Dozens of people, most of them children, witness the attack. In their terror, they throw themselves flat on their bellies in the mud.

Umar, the girls' father, is on his way home from work when he hears the shots. He races to Larissa's side and tries to carry her to his car. But the same soldier fires a second round at the young woman, then a third, which hits her squarely in the chest. She dies several moments later. "While I was holding her, after the first shots, she whispered to me, 'Papa, go; if you don't, they're going to shoot you,'" Umar Ketiev recounts. His eyes are just a little red. As is the custom in the Caucasus, he is making an effort not to show his sorrow in public.

The next day, at dawn, Umar assembles his eight surviving children (six girls and two boys), Larissa's coffin, and members of the family living in or near Sleptsovskii. They are going to the village of Iandyrka, to the house where Larissa's mother was born. In keeping with tradition, Larissa will be buried on family ground.

Pink sheets are hanging over a laundry line in the snowy courtyard of the little blue cottage at 21 Lenin Street. Twenty or thirty persons fill the only room, heated by a stove. Bread and hot tea are offered to each new arrival. Carpets have been hung on the cold walls. Umar and his wife sit at a table, their hands joined atop the red plastic tablecloth. The girls stay in the background, sitting on the ground or the window ledges. Larissa is remembered as someone who had hoped to study law but who had devoted herself instead to her family's survival: "She was the one who fed all of us, who bought our clothes," Madina says, stifling her sobs. Lida, hidden behind her headscarf, remains silent as she leans against the wall.

Umar, who doesn't hide his displeasure when the women or girls display their emotions, clears his throat before speaking. He is dressed in a gray coat and hat. "I've brought my children up with a moral sense. They're all good children. My two sons even served in the Russian army, the same one that took our daughter from us." Then, moved but maintaining his dignity, he draws from the pocket of his ragged coat a typed letter protected by a plastic sleeve. It is a letter of apology from the Minister of Defense. "This won't bring our daughter back to us, but still I'm grateful to them for their response. We were even astonished by it; we had thought that the crime would go unpunished." In his black-bordered letter, the Russian minister explains that financial aid will be given to the family and that the guilty parties, already under arrest, will no doubt be given the maximum sentence of life in prison. He offers his apologies for this "deplorable error."

Lyubov, Larissa's mother, a former milkmaid on a Soviet farm and an ex-deputy of the Supreme Soviet of the Republic of Chechno-Ingushetia, is huddled under her shawl. She manages to hide her sorrow. But if her husband seems determined not to speak ill of the Russians, she is more spontaneous and also more critical: "Those soldiers were drunk, but they didn't kill Larissa because she refused to sell them vodka. They didn't even ask her if she had any vodka. She was a beautiful girl, my Larissa!" She draws a dog-eared photo out from underneath her skirts. The little girl in the picture looks charming as she glances at the photographer out of the corner of her eye. "I'd just like to say a few words to the mother of the man who shot her. How did she bring up her son? It wasn't milk she gave him as a baby to nurse on, it was poison. I'd like to wring his neck." All around me the eyes of the onlookers are red and swollen, but no one is crying. That's not allowed, especially in the presence of strangers. "Such a thing could never, in any case, have happened in the days of the Soviet

Union," Lyubov continues. "Under the Soviets there were no tragedies of this kind, or people were punished right then and there. Or rather we punished them ourselves; that was the quickest way."

The family's rage is focused on the murderer, who, it turns out, is Ossetian, not Russian. Larissa, however, was Ingush. In this region, shared by a number of peoples, ethnic tensions result in frequent clashes. Before the first Russo-Chechen war, in 1994, the southern flank of Ingushetia had been the scene of violent territorial disputes between the Ossetians and the Ingush. The event that touched off the confrontations was the 1992 assassination of a young Ingush woman by the Ossetians. Umar cannot ignore the similarity: "They came to carry out the same operation all over again. Up until now, when they came to the kiosk, not one soldier brought his gun with him. This one really wanted to kill my daughter because she was Ingush. But we're not going to respond to this provocation, and we're not afraid of them because we belong to the Russian Federation. There are many people who would like to fight this war on Ingush territory, too, but we'll have none of that!"

"I don't agree. I think that the Russians are capable of anything," another sister from Grozny speaks up. Then she buries her face in her scarf to hide her tears.

Her father shoots her an angry look. He continues stubbornly, "Our elders taught us to forgive, and so we have forgiven. And we still listen to our president."

A man comes in and whispers something in Umar's ear. Umar gets up. "I must go to another burial," he says.

Only the women are left. They recite prayers in a corner of the room. They will have to wait for the seventh day after the burial to visit Larissa's grave because, according to custom, the ritual of the burial is exclusively for males. They'll kill a cow and a goat on that day, and there will be a veritable banquet for all the members of the family.

The light is growing dim, and it's time to leave. We exchange furtive smiles, despite the solemnity of the occasion. Two of the sisters, Lida, who was present in the kiosk on the day of the shooting, and Assia, her younger sister, ask me if they can ride with us to Sleptsovskii "to see if everything is all right in the kiosk." They scarcely say goodbye to their family. I wonder how they're going to get back and tell myself to leave them with a little money for a taxi. When we're on our way, the tears flow down their cheeks. "We try to hold them back in front of our parents, and they do the same," says Lida with a sniffle, "but I know that, when the two of them are by themselves, it's another story."

The wooden kiosk is barricaded and padlocked. We reach it by tramping through the mud. Lida and Assia manage to worm their way in; they rummage about loudly and leave again, satisfied.

Lida has one more thing to say on the subject of Larissa: "That Thursday morning, a passerby bought a soda from us and told us that he had lost his father in an accident in Ossetia. Larissa told me five or six times over 'I'm not going to die. I want to live! I have so many things I want to do!'"

Over our heads the planes are roaring in the direction of Chechnya. In a few minutes from now, more people, over there, are going to die.

Clothesline has been strung between the windows of the green and yellow railroad car and the trees lining the track. Every ten meters or so little groups of men are squatting around a brazier made from rusted iron. In front of each wagon is a small wooden outhouse. Outside Sleptsovskii, in the middle of a plain with the Caucasus mountains for a backdrop, dozens of these cars have been parked on an abandoned spur next to an ancient cemetery. Hundreds of Chechen refugees without family or friends in Ingushetia have settled here. Some have been here for three months.

Timur, a construction worker, has recognized Islam in the front seat of the car. He climbs in beside me in the rear. He comes from Urus-Martan, which has been under Russian fire for several days now, but he managed to escape the worst. He is small with blue eyes and a lost expression. He wears an old tight-fitting leather jacket, and his hands are filthy. He is ill at ease in Russian, which he hasn't learned for the simple reason that he never went to school. He prefers to speak with Islam in Chechen, but from time to time I interrupt to ask a question in Russian.

"I have nothing left, no house, no cow. I abandoned everything back there. I left with two cars chock-full—two women and eight children. When we got here, where were we supposed to go? What was I supposed to do with them? Put them in the railway cars? In the tent camp at Karabulak? Finally, I managed to find shelter for them in four different places."

Beside us, three old men are playing cards on a colored tea towel spread out on the ground. Children are sawing wood. Timur continues, "Yesterday, I had nothing but a cup of tea all day. I have no money. I spent all of it on buses. What's more, at the border, we had to wait hours, just because we didn't have any money to pay for our crossing. They took my cigarettes, my lighter, and a bottle of perfume."

Timur invites us into "his" railway car. Several families are squished in here. One seat is often shared by four or even five persons. Inside, the berths are stacked three high and separated by flimsy partitions. Everyone "owns" his little bit of the aisle. We take off our shoes before entering.

Riamzan is the "chief" of Wagon 110. The fifty other occupants of the car chose him because he was one of the first to arrive, at the beginning of October. He complains in a calm voice about the continual difficulties he faces in trying to improve daily life for his fellow refugees.

"First, the windows are terribly drafty—the cars are Soviet-made—and we have had to plug them up with mattress stuffing. Then we had to organize ourselves in teams to bring water from two and a half kilometers away. The nights are cold, but the authorities refuse to give us a second blanket. Every day I go to the Federal Immigration Service to plead our cause."

A pile of coal in a corner will be used to fire the car's boiler, which was originally used to make tea for the passengers. "That boiler threatens to explode at any moment. It makes us all terribly afraid," Riamzan remarks. A woman goes by, pushing a five-year-old before her. She is wearing a long flowered summer dress without sleeves. "It's all she was able to take with her. Her indoor clothes. She doesn't even have a coat."

The lady in question, Zura, arrived the previous day with her three children, having walked fifty kilometers in three days and three nights. She had to wait more than forty-eight hours at the border crossing, where they let the refugees in only one by one. She is still in shock; her eyes are haggard and her talk disjointed. Her son, Makhmud, who is "a little deranged because he has never known anything but war," never stops making faces and scratching his head nervously.

Slowly, with great effort, Zura begins to describe the horror she left behind. "When I was little, we used to watch films about the Great Patriotic War* on television. We lived through the same thing at Urus-Martan. It was merciless. The worst were the helicopters. They flew so low that we could see the faces of our killers. For a week they bombed us on a grid pattern, methodically."

What convinced her to leave?

"During the raid I thought I was going to die. I scarcely had time to reach the cellar where we spent our days and nights. I felt as though I had been swept up in a burning heat wave. I lost consciousness."

Zura's right side is covered with burns; she is in pain, but has not been able to see a doctor. She doesn't know where to turn, because there is no medical help provided for the seventeen cars.

I ask her why she and her family stayed on so long in Urus-

---

* For the Russians, the war against Hitler's Germany after the renunciation of the Hitler-Stalin Pact.

Martan when most of the other residents had left the city at the beginning of November.

"No one ever thought that it would go this far," she answers. "During the last war, we were declared a 'refugee zone.' I had twenty-five refugees in my house. We didn't see one plane. Now, if I had the money, I'd leave Russia; there is no more hope here. And yet, after the first war, we thought we'd be able to live in peace. Some people even rebuilt their houses from top to bottom."

Zura can't stop thinking about those she left behind: "All the houses were destroyed, without exception. After us, nobody could be left there. Everybody must be dead. Bodies were laid out everywhere in the streets. Wild dogs were eating them."

I ask Zura whether the Russians might have attacked Urus-Martan so viciously because it was reputed to be a Wahhabi base. "Of course, we knew these Wahhabis, and no one liked them," she replies. "At least, not in my street. And we would certainly have pointed out to the Russians where they lived, but we were the ones they targeted," she says accusingly, in a voice that has recovered some of its strength. "The Wahhabis were already in Urus-Martan during the first war, but they were more discreet, and there were fewer of them. Since then, they've taken over everything—the hospitals, the schools. The power was in their hands. It was very unpleasant to live with them; they wanted all the women to veil themselves, to wear long skirts. When someone made a little money, they would come to his house to ask for some or they'd make him pay tribute in weapons."

She adds, "Since the end of the Soviet Union and this independence movement, we've lived in continual fear. Fear of the Russians and of the Wahhabis."

Silence. Then she begins again: "It was under Dudayev that we became poor. I was a seamstress in a factory, and my husband was a mason. If we have to pay the price of this independence with our blood, then I'm not for it, and I don't want to have anything to do with it. We won't go back to our country until we can be sure that the bombing has stopped for good. We'll live in a cave; we're already used to it. In any case, it took us twenty-two years to build our house, and I haven't the strength to start again. We've lived under the Russians, and we know what to expect."

Makhmud has stopped grimacing. Now he is trembling with cold, and he tugs at his mother's hand, pulling her toward the warmth of the treacherous boiler.

⌒

Islam has a fever and cannot accompany me to Chechnya this time. But he has found me a remote relative, a refugee named Zarema, who needs to go to Achkhoy-Martan to attend to family business. We agree to meet early the next morning at the Kavkaz border crossing, where we'll take a bus or commandeer a private car in exchange for a fistful of rubles.

The line of vehicles extends for several kilometers along the muddy road. Gray cars and a few yellow minibuses—flying makeshift white flags or rags tied to their windshields or rearview mirrors—splatter the passers-by without pity. Most of the rags are not white, but gray. But nobody seems to notice the difference. At last a private car picks us up; but then we wait, inching forward in single file. Near the barrier that constitutes the frontier, television crews are filming the cars. I lower my head and readjust my head-scarf so that I pass unnoticed. Sometimes the men scan the sky, watching the airplanes overhead. The young people argue about what to do for their country's future. Some are adamant about the need to stay put; only then will they be able to help their own people. It's a refrain I hear constantly from Islam. For others, the best course is to flee with their families to another country. But where? Which country accepts Chechen refugees?

The wildest rumors circulate about what may happen. One of the most persistent has the Russians using chemical weapons against Grozny. The capital will disappear entirely into the earth; all those who have had the misfortune to stay there will be buried. According to this rumor, another capital will then be constructed somewhat to the north, on the southern bank of the Terek River.

Tanks are stationed on either side of the asphalt road. We sometimes spot their long guns sticking out from behind the bushes. Suddenly, two soldiers appear out of nowhere and pull a sheep out of the truck just in front of us. The soldiers head off across the fields, dragging the animal by its neck. The heavy vehicle jerks into motion, passes the line of waiting cars, and grows faint in the distance, leaving a trail of fumes behind it. Other buses that have paid to avoid the wait also pass us, but the driver of our car refuses to play this game. "Out of principle," he says. "Otherwise they'll recognize me afterwards and try to make me pay at every checkpoint. I don't have enough money for that."

I want to give him a few bills and thus spare us the wait, but this will tip him off that I am a foreigner. Out of the corner of her eye, Zarema signals to me to do nothing. Sometimes, to allay suspicions, she addresses some words to me in Chechen, and I respond by laughing and shrugging my shoulders. Otherwise, I keep silent.

At last we reach the militiamen. They make the two men get out of the car but don't pay the slightest attention to us. Along the side of the road, swarms of birds swoop out of the trees and flutter along a little way. We're back in Chechnya, once again on the Rostov-Baku highway, the principal axis that cuts Chechnya in two.

In this territory, occupied at present by the Russians, the atmosphere is very different; for some reason, I feel much less safe here. During my travels, the rebel-held territory has become smaller and smaller. At the same time, it's getting more and more difficult to pass through the Russian positions. It's all mixed up. This time I'm not going to stay long. I'm only going to stop in Achkhoy-Martan, at Magomed's, to find out what has happened there. Is he still alive? How is the Russian occupation going?

Our driver stops to pick up some hitchhikers along the route. I sit in Zarema's lap and put my arms around her shoulders. It's as though she's my big sister, which is what we have agreed to say if we are questioned.

The Russian troops are concealed on either side of the asphalt highway. Their positions are scarcely visible through the damp, milk-like fog. Here and there, however, a trail of smoke emerging from the treetops signals one of their camps. Tank tracks in the mud disfigure the landscape, as do the half-topped trees along the roadside. Some of the trees lie in the road, only half sawn-through, as though some important event had caused the perpetrator of the ecological "crime" to change his mind. This sense of unfinished business makes me uneasy.

There are many checkpoints; the first, as we enter Assinovskii, another as we leave, others on the way to Achkhoy-Martan. Very young Russians are on duty. It's always the same scenario: The soldiers make the men get out of the car and search them or check their identity papers. Depending on their humor or their zeal, the soldiers then check the trunk. If the trunk is empty—as it is in our case—they search for something else on which to levy duty. One of them asks our driver, "What have you got in the way of cassettes?"

"Russian music," the Chechen answers.

"What kind? Oldies or modern?"

"Modern."

"Give it to us. It's kind of boring here."

But if the trunk is full of goods—which is often the case, because many *spekulianty* ("speculators") ply the route between Ingushetia and the Chechen villages to supply the markets—the soldiers help themselves. A sort of payment in kind.

A little farther along, we are asked to lend a hand with the breakdown of a "local" whose battery has failed. We have no choice but to agree. We usually encounter the Russian soldiers in twos and threes, slumped on the small hillocks of earth they threw up as they dug their trenches. The fields are covered with these giant molehills. The young men have little to keep them busy. They're following orders but dying of boredom.

$$\triangle$$

Something awful has happened in the market of Achkhoy-Martan. The improvised stalls with their plastic-sheet roofing, which sold the usual—toothpaste, cookies, tea, instant coffee—are now in ruins. Bits of wood litter the slippery ground. Thirty or so women in rubber boots are wading about in the mud. The night before, Russian soldiers amused themselves by destroying everything in sight. Lida, wrapped in her headscarf, tells the story reluctantly: "They don't come here very often, but yesterday, at about five in the afternoon, a Russian BTR* appeared. They wanted to trade their grenade launcher for four bottles of vodka. But we didn't have any vodka here. We don't drink. We're Muslims.... They were all blind drunk, and we just had to stand back and let them go at it."

After suffering intense bombing during most of October, the population of this small town west of Grozny is still reeling from the shock of the Russians' arrival. Without water or gas or electricity since the beginning of the Russian offensive, Achkhoy-Martan "surrendered" in mid-November. The community, which is essentially agricultural, had no one at all to defend it.

The almost deserted streets are lined with brick houses behind high closed gates; a few women carrying plastic or tin buckets are

---

* Armored car.

fetching water from the well. Young people with nothing else to do stand about, their hands in their pockets, wool caps pulled over their ears, and watch the cars go by. There's not a lot for them to see because gas is so rare and so expensive.

On the grayish central square stands a group of old men; each has a *papakha* on his head and a cane in his hand. Not a single Russian in sight. "They haven't really entered our town," Sharib Arsamikov explains. An entire wall of his house is being rebuilt after three shells landed in his courtyard a few days ago. "For the moment they're being discreet, staying on the outskirts."

The rapport between the Russian troops and the population of Achkhoy-Martan is confused. For now, the Federal troops are massed just outside the town. Russian media have reported that the "older townspeople" helped "surrender" the town. That is not the universally agreed upon version of events.

"We were at a dead end," Zalaudin Dzhevatkhanov, one of the nine inhabitants who participated in the negotiations, explains. "Our town was completely surrounded; the population was panicking. A Chechen from Moscow offered to mediate. He informed us by telegram that he was ready to come to aid us in the talks. We accepted, and the town was behind us."

Daud Salayev, another senior citizen, doesn't agree: "I, for example, was never informed about these negotiations. No one ever asked me to participate, because they know my feelings toward the Russians. I haven't changed my position since the first war."

At Achkhoy-Martan, as elsewhere in Chechnya, two layers of authority appear to be superimposed one on another. The official layer is exercised by the prefect of the region on behalf of the president, Aslan Maskhadov; the unofficial authority is exercised by the inhabitants grouped according to the *teip* (in Chechen) or *rod* (in Russian)—that is, the clan each one belongs to. In the clans, ties of blood take precedence over all others. To deal with the situation on November 6, 1999, Achkhoy-Martan set up a "coordinating committee" of nine men who enjoyed a certain influence in the village, either because of their service in the local administration or their leadership in the agricultural sector during the Soviet era. It is universally agreed that the Soviets do not keep their word. After the visit of General Vladimir Shamanov, then commander of the western front, who negotiated the surrender in exchange for an end to the bombing, the artillery strikes redoubled in intensity. Seven more people were killed and a hundred more houses were destroyed.

"And yet he had given us his word as a general: 'Not one shell will fall on you, and we will open the road to Valerik, a nearby town,'" Zalaudin Dzhevatkhanov testifies. He is standing, in baggy trousers and house slippers, in the courtyard of his house. "Then they apologized and explained that they had mixed us up with Bamut! Can you imagine such a farce! I have no windows left since that infamous night when they turned everything loose on us!" The yawning openings let the cold in. Zalaudin has nailed bits of transparent plastic to the window frames, but it's still frigid.

Three houses away, I visit with Iussa Beksultanov. His hair and eyebrows are tousled because he has just woken up: "Here there is nothing else to do but lie down and wait, and try to sleep in order to forget."

Iussa is the vice prefect of the region, and, like most of those he administers, he seems to have lost all hope. "We surrendered to the Russians because we weren't prepared to defend ourselves," he concedes, "and it wasn't even worth our trouble to try. Here, no one is fighting for Chechen independence, and the Russians know that very well. They're taking advantage of our weariness. Our people are scared, they're hungry, and they'll support almost any-one."

He continues with a sigh: "Building a state is always difficult. The one we inherited in 1996 was in ruins. No one would have been able to raise it from the ashes. For my part, I believed in the peace accord signed with Yeltsin in 1997. I was disappointed. But we are not blameless; in three years we have accomplished noth-ing! That's the fault of the bad management policies of Maskhadov."

It's clear that in Achkhoy-Martan, the dream of an independ-ent "Ichkeria" has been largely abandoned. "In order to survive," Iussa says, "Chechnya needs a strong state. With or without Rus-sia. But until now we have not been recognized by any other country that I know of."

From time to time, guns sound in the distance. On every street corner, control posts have been set up by the inhabitants, who want to observe the comings and goings of their neighbors. The residents are lying low in their houses and counting on the fingers of one hand the sacks of flour and sugar they have left.

"All the politics are going on behind our backs," Iussa con-cludes. "Neither the Russians nor the Chechen leaders have ever asked the Chechen people for advice. So we suffer in silence."

Once more—this time in the company of Zarema—I am back at Magomed's, close to the stove; it's so hot that my head spins when I leave the room.

The master of the house is lucky to still have his wife, his son, and his six daughters with him. Because of this, his lips form a permanent smile. Aza recognizes me the moment I enter the courtyard. She seems happy to see me.

Aza's older sister, the twenty-one-year-old Luisa, has been married for three years to a man ten years her senior. They live in the house across the street. While we squat in a corner of the courtyard so that I can smoke a cigarette—in Chechnya, women don't smoke—Luisa suddenly confides that she is very unhappy because her father has forced her to marry this young man from a "rich family." She tells me that her husband is a drug addict (*narkoman*). When I ask her more about it, she refuses to elaborate.

"As for the family's money, I never see any of it," she tells me in a childish, but disappointed tone. "They keep everything for themselves and never give me anything." This is the reason she spends her time on this side of the street with her parents and her other sisters, though custom decrees that she live with her in-laws and her baby, Imal. "What great things I could have done, if only I hadn't married!" she laments. "In the first place, I would have finished my studies at the institute; and I would have become a journalist like you and would have traveled all over the world. It's a wonderful career, isn't it? You only see beautiful things. But now it's too late for me."

I remark that the "beautiful things" I have witnessed in my career include the war in her country. This gives her pause.

Luisa talks almost in a laughing tone; I suppose that if she didn't take life lightly, her existence would be a veritable hell.

Inside the house, Aza is no longer at the stove. Her older sister, Rita, is formally in charge of the household now that Luisa has married. This responsibility will pass from daughter to daughter as each one marries. When a Chechen family is large and there are many daughters, the mother has a labor force that she draws on to take care of her sons. For the perpetuation of the *teip*, of course, it's always better to have sons.

Magomed talks nonstop, but his wife is silent. He is pleased to have made the acquaintance of Zarema. Perhaps they will be able to set up a little commerce between Ingushetia and Achkhoy-Martan.

≙

At Assinovskii, not far from the frontier with Ingushetia, on the Chechen side of the border, everyone worries that the evacuation corridor for refugees from the war zone will be closed permanently. Right now, arbitrary closures occur throughout the day, without rhyme or reason. Night and day, the line of cars extends over more than three kilometers. The passengers in the cars, tractors, vans, and buses are accustomed to waiting patiently. They sit there, studying the smallest sign or gesture on the part of the border guards at the Kavkaz crossing, a hundred meters away. Zarema and I are taken by surprise; the taxi that brought us from Achkhoy-Martan dropped us here, then turned around and left us. We're on foot in the mud.

Dusk is approaching. Only the mooing of a cow breaks the silence. The owner has thrown a blanket over the cow's young calf, and the two animals are taking the air in the back of a small truck. The calf is chewing innocently at the white rag attached to the truck as a flag of peace. A group of men and women, all chilled through and dirty, are camped permanently in front of the hastily installed barbed wire barrier that marks the limit beyond which no one can pass. We join the group. There, we are able to make out a hand-written sign: "Attention: Frontier post. Anyone passing beyond this limit will be fired upon."

Among the people waiting is a peasant woman from Urus-Martan. She's standing in the snow squall, holding a plastic bag in each hand. Loud squawks are coming from the bags. By clicking her tongue and shaking the sacks, she manages to quiet whatever is inside. I finally identify the contents as two hens. The two fowl —all that she possesses in the world—are accompanying her on her border-crossing adventure. "At Urus-Martan, we've been living in caves for ten days. It's been impossible to stick your nose out of doors; they're bombing all the time," she tells me. Her solution is to try to reunite with part of her family, refugees somewhere near Nazran in Ingushetia, and to get what money she can from the sale of the two "survivors" of her hen house.

But, today, we shouldn't kid ourselves; the peasant woman won't cross, and neither will we. The Russians have just closed the border for the day. We will all need to find somewhere to sleep. It is ten minutes past one in the afternoon when a khaki army jeep covers the hundred meters separating the Russian post from the perplexed but silent crowd. "Closed!" a soldier calls out. The reason? There isn't one. "Orders," answers the soldier, who can't be more than eighteen. The jeep drives off, leaving behind hundreds of angry men and women. Still, not a single vehicle turns around. No one is willing to give up his place in the line.

A taxi driver from Argun, forty kilometers from Grozny, who is still dizzy from the noise of the constant bombing of his town, groans despairingly: "It's exactly the same as yesterday. They close the border because they want to make money. Mornings they can hit the people in line for a thousand rubles [$40, an exorbitant sum for a Chechen], but after lunch they'll take only greenbacks. It's generally $100 a person. Then nobody gets through. But we have nothing else to do but wait, just in case."

Zarema is furious, because her daughter is waiting for her on the other side. "Maybe she'll think of sending someone over to help get us out of here," she muses aloud. I think this is unlikely.

Around five o'clock, at dusk, oil lamps appear here and there in the cars. Some drivers run their motors periodically to try to generate a little heat. By the roadside, the local "speculators" continue to do business. They roast mutton on improvised barbecues stoked with branches from the surrounding trees—all stripped bare up to the height of a man. They serve tea in plastic glasses. The only light and noise come from the headlights and the engines of the Russian army vehicles, the only ones now allowed to move freely about on the highway.

From time to time, an armored carrier slows down and parks in the mud by the roadside. Two or three soldiers get out and approach the speculators. "Often they pretend that they don't have enough money to pay us, and they more or less make us give them biscuits or chocolate at reduced prices. What can we do? They're like us, they're hungry!" Radima Merzhueva, a fifty-four-year-old seller, says sympathetically.

Before getting back in his vehicle, one of the soldiers cautiously approaches the old man with whom Zarema and I are conversing under a tree. By chance, the young Russian addresses his remarks to me. "Excuse me, Miss, but do you know where we can find some vodka around here?" he asks, embarrassed. In a panic, I step backwards and slip on the mud.

Zarema grabs my sleeve, preventing me from falling down flat, and answers in my place: "You won't find a single bottle on this road. Sorry!"

A few minutes later, a third soldier tries, hesitantly, for the last time: "Would you like some cheap gasoline? We'll trade you as much as you like for alcohol and biscuits."

Negative response from the old Chechen. The armored car starts up and disappears into the night.

Several seconds later, we hear the sharp rattle of a Kalachnikov followed by the hoarse shouts of a soldier. "Halt! Stop! One more step and I fire!" Three women, who had decided to advance on the post in hopes of crossing on foot and without baggage, scurry back to where they came from. I convince Zarema that we should leave the road and search for shelter. From memory, I lead her to

Akhmed's abandoned house where we stopped with Islam some weeks before. It's farther away than I thought, and the kilometers we have to walk seem long in the blackness.

We will have to wait at least another fifteen hours, until around 10:00 A.M. the next morning, when the corridor will be reopened to the waiting crowd.

Chapter 5

A s HE WAS HEADING for Ingushetia, Solzbek left his weapons for safe keeping on the Chechen side of the frontier. He plans to pick them up on his way back to Grozny. Although the Russian ultimatum*will expire in forty-eight hours, Solzbek is one of only a few who have been able to reach Ingushetia from the besieged capital.

In front of the Kavkaz checkpoint, a crowd of reporters and residents has gathered, the latter hoping to spot relatives or friends in the expected flood of new refugees. For the moment, nothing. A representative of the Ministry of the Interior is standing near a slab of concrete, waving a piece of paper with the registration

---

* In December 1999, the Russian troops issued an ultimatum to the inhabitants of Grozny. By Saturday, December 11, all inhabitants had to leave the town by corridors going northwestward, in the direction of Ingushetia.

numbers of cars authorized to pass into Chechnya. For the most part, these are only vehicles of the Ministry of Emergencies, whose head, Sergei Shoygu, is expected to arrive at any moment. The post is unusually calm in the slanting rays of sunshine.

Last Tuesday, Solzbek left Grozny in two cars, together with nine companions, all part of the same battle unit. "I have important business here," he confides mysteriously. "As soon as it's finished, I'll go back to Grozny." It took the group four days to reach Sleptsovskii, in Ingushetia. Even though he's a rebel fighter, Solzbek, who holds a valid internal passport,* had no trouble crossing the frontier.

"Getting out of Grozny is the hard part," he explains. "Even for the civilians it's incredibly difficult. The roads are very dangerous. In fact, I didn't see a single regular bus operating. No one knows where the Russians are, or if they'll fire. There have been many reported cases of shootings. What's more, many people would like to leave, but they just don't have the means. People there have become indifferent to their own fate."

As for the ultimatum offering safe corridors for departure, supposedly announced in leaflets dropped by planes, Solzbek has never heard of it: "In the various parts of Grozny where I have been operating recently, no one—neither civilians nor combatants, like me—has any means of receiving information from the outside. There's no television, and I rarely meet anyone who even has a radio."

---

* For travel within the confines of the Russian Federation, citizens must be in possession of a so-called internal passport; they must apply for an external passport for travel outside the Federation.

Solzbek, like the vast majority of other refugees, took the southern route out of Grozny, which is 90 percent surrounded by Russian troops. But, "at Prigorodny [a southern suburb], we were afraid of running into the Russians. So we cut our lights and we reconnoitered on foot. The snipers were aiming for us, but we just managed to get through in the car. The Russians," he continues, "aren't very mobile. Once they get a post set up, they're very reluctant to leave it, especially at night."

The two cars then headed for Urus-Martan, which had been taken by the Russians shortly before. The town was in ruins. "We slept in abandoned houses, and there were plenty to choose from. There's almost no one left besides soldiers. Everything was destroyed, sacked. Mattresses and even rolled-up rugs were piled up on BTRs. What the Russians can't carry away—large pieces of furniture, for example—they simply smash up. The Russian commander was walking around among the ruins with lists of houses belonging to the rebels or their families. They torch them."

In Urus-Martan there are also troops under the command of the pro-Russian Chechen leader, Bislan Gantemirov, a former mayor of Grozny. Gantemirov was convicted of embezzlement in 1996, but Moscow recently released him, in the hopes that he will help them with the situation in Chechnya. "I asked one of his men, who was wearing a white armband, who his enemies were," Solzbek recounts. "'Anyone who attacks me,' he said. 'And if your attackers address you with an *Allah Akhbar,* what will you say?' He didn't answer. He just walked away. I was ashamed for him," Solzbek comments.

Solzbek looks much older than his nineteen years. His face is careworn and his features drawn; he wears an old leather jacket and a black wool cap that he never takes off, even inside, where it's warm. "I'm going to bring back some canned goods to Grozny," he says, "for the women on my street. There are still many left, with children." His own family has been living for two months in Sernovodsk, a Chechen village close to the Ingushetia frontier. He will stop by to see them on his way home. To hear him tell it, village life, such as it is, continues under the Russian assault, though the market now consists of no more than a dozen measly stalls selling bread, soda, candles, and flashlights.

"We've had enough of waiting for the Russians," the rebel fighter explains. "No one in the city thinks that they'll really get in. Sure, we're letting them take the outlying areas, which may give the impression that we're losing speed. But it's quite the opposite. Each side is fighting with what he has. They have air power and artillery; we have direct confrontation. We'll force them into close combat."

It's a day like all the others at the Kavkaz border crossing. "We're waiting for our relatives as usual, and, as usual, they're not coming," says Lida, who is up to her ankles in mud, as she waits with the crowd. This Saturday, only three buses and four cars have arrived from Chechnya. In the outbound direction, the traffic is moving along faster, to the great satisfaction of the representatives of the Ministry of the Interior. "There are three times more cars leaving for Chechnya," Riamzan, a sergeant of Ingush origin, brags. "And that's very good. That means that the refugees are going home. They're no longer afraid to go back to the territories in the hands of Federal forces."

Miraculously, we encounter no problems crossing the border. Islam has found a car in Kavkaz that will take us as far as Urus-Martan. For once, there is no inspection at all. In the milky fog, we meet only the jeeps of the MtchS (Ministry for Emergencies) as we pass though Assinovskii, and I note that there's still the same long line of cars in the opposite direction. Islam pulls his Reebok cap down around his ears, a rallying sign for the *boyviki* in rebel territory.

Tractors are working in the fields. Cowherds armed with clubs steer their herds. Horse-drawn carts piled high with wood grind along the side of the road. Winter is already upon us, and it looks as if it will be a hard one.

The car is stopped for the first time just before Achkhoy-Martan. This is something new. The soldiers who search us are Ossetian, but they speak a little bit of Russian, which shocks Islam. One of them opens the car door on my side and asks me if I have presented my papers to his colleagues. In my surprise—because this is also the first time such a thing has happened—I answer yes without thinking. The lie saves me: The soldier lets us pass without checking.

There's more life in Achkhoy-Martan than the last time we were here. Cans of adulterated gasoline are being sold along the roadside. There are wood fires, groups of men at the intersections, women working bent over in the fields. At the entrance to the village of Kotel Yurt, a member of the Gantemirov militia signals us to stop for a control. Islam asks me, amused, whether the soldier has "the look of a real *boyvik.*" He'd like me to be able to tell the difference, as he can.

"It's a bit difficult to know just from their physical appearance," I reply.

At Valerik, traffic becomes a problem because the road is bad and the market is very active. Tanker trucks of water are trying to squeeze through the streets. Dump trucks full of wood are parked everywhere, blocking the way. The price of wood is high, of course, because those who chopped and gathered it did so at the risk of their lives. A women sits knitting quietly as the cars slalom around the enormous potholes full of water. She is selling macaroni. The nostrils of a horse are giving off steam in a curious cone shape that resembles, strangely enough, the load he's pulling. A column of six armored cars passes without drawing comment. It's true: I had forgotten for a moment that we were in "liberated" territory. Islam has a funny expression. He says little, but I guess that he feels ill at ease. He can't wait to get back to "the other side."

At the entrance to Urus-Martan, we come upon disaster. The kiosks in the market have been flattened, most of the houses are destroyed, some of them are still burning. Ragged curtains hang at windows without panes. The impact of shells has traced macabre designs on every vertical surface. The sound of gunfire vibrates through the air. We are only twenty kilometers south of Grozny.

Islam is searching for a friend who will put us up for the night. We walk for a long time through the ruins of Urus-Martan while he tries to remember the way. We cross a small suspension bridge over a body of water littered with the carcasses of cars. There is even a rusted BTR: "It goes back to the first war," Islam tells me. Roosters are crowing even though it's almost evening. Everything is out of kilter. On a gust of wind, the acrid odor of charred bodies wafts our way. Bones are still smoking in the ashes of a fire. I have a feeling of foreboding. We walk on.

We find the house at last, but it is empty. "They left not very long ago," Islam tells me. "I wonder how they got out." An old television set is abandoned in the middle of a windowless room. Shell holes pock the walls, shards of glass are strewn over the floor. The cupboards are empty; some are tipped over. The inhabitants of the house must have left in a great hurry. A few plastic flowers are still fixed to one of the walls. A strap from a handbag forms a curl on the floor. Wood is stacked and abandoned in the courtyard.

Every day we have to worry about where we're going to sleep that evening. This time, we've come up empty-handed, but we still have several hours before darkness falls. We'll find something. I have confidence in Islam and in all these Chechens who, despite their misery, remain so hospitable. They have nothing, yet they offer me everything.

We double back and head for the center of town. The people we pass are listless, dazed even. A few of them are busy reconstructing their houses. As usual, the women are performing all the domestic chores. To my amazement, I hear the whine of an electric saw, operated no doubt by some lucky person with his own generator. Although the Russian attack is over and the town is already reviving, some of the old people are still hiding in their cellars; they refuse to come out for fear of what they'll find above ground. No one feels safe any longer.

We arrive in the center, not far from the spot—already dis-
cernible—where the Russians will install their *kommandantura*.* A
cluster of people has gathered around a wrecked car. There are
some Chechens and one or two Russians, including an angry
official who is gesturing wildly. "I warn you," the chief shouts.
"The next time you see someone film something without authori-
zation or any type of journalist taking notes, I demand that you
denounce him! Don't miss out! You'll be rewarded for your civic
spirit!" I laugh to myself, imagining what would happen if the
officer knew who I was and what I had already recorded en route.

Islam is visibly ill at ease. He glances at me meaningfully and
starts to move away from the group. I stay on a moment, amused
by the situation. From what I understand, earlier in the day a BTR
crashed into a car, killing its two civilian occupants. A television
crew from the Russian private channel NTV, who happened to be
passing through Urus-Martan, was alerted to what had happened
by a "local" and came to film the aftermath. "I ought to view all
the cassettes that are made in this country," rants the Russian
official.

We linger on the central square, trying to decide what to do
next. I am buying some oranges—a rare luxury—and some Snickers from a stall when I spot Islam getting into a car parked near the
taxi stand. Once more he has met up with an old acquaintance—
Chechnya is small, the circles of friendship there are large—a man
by the name of Suslansbek, who invites us to spend the night with
him in the village of Shaami Yurt.

---

* Headquarters of the police of the Russian occupying forces.

"If we can get safely to Shaami Yurt, we won't need to worry about the rest; it will all be fine!" Suslansbek assures us, laughing. He is only repeating the words of a Russian officer. He is a taxi driver, and the father of three daughters, a son, and another child on the way. He is both proud and embarrassed for his home town. "It seems that the Russians remembered our village from the first war," he says. "So easy to take, so pleasant to live in, without a single defender!"

Suslansbek is the last son in a family of six children whose roots go back to the village's beginnings. After the first Russo-Chechen war, his three brothers returned to their professional lives in Grozny, and his two sisters, also married with children, moved away from the family home. This second war has brought the family back together, but without the good relations that prevailed during the earlier conflict. "Operation Antiterrorist" has split the family down the middle, making political discussion almost impossible. The two older sons, Ruslan and Aslanbek, are hostile to even the idea of independence, but the two younger sons, Nazarbek and Suslansbek, support the war and the rebel cause. This argument separates the generation that lived under the Soviet Union before the first war from those who came of age with the idea of an independent "Ichkeria" under Dzhokhar Dudayev. Ruslan, the oldest, is particularly resentful of Aslan Maskhadov. "We really thought he would be a good president," he says. "But he committed many errors. Obviously, he was terrified of the Wahhabis, of Bassayev, and others. But if he were a true Muslim, he absolutely would not have been afraid of them!"

Aslanbek, his younger brother, elaborates: "Maskhadov simply sat around with his arms crossed. All these kidnappings—he knows perfectly well who's in charge of carrying them out, but he does nothing. He's a weakling. And his entourage is even worse. All the appointments in the administration have been made in the same way: They hired only people who had fought, in order to recompense them in some way. All others were and are considered second-class citizens. We've had enough of this war!"

Then, in a lower voice he adds, "If the Russians stay here and don't do anything to us, we'll be forced to accept them. You have to look things squarely in the eye; what can we do against the Russians?"

Nazarbek does not share this opinion; he was a member of the department of political analysis in the Dudayev government between 1994 and 1995, and then served Dudayev's successor, Zelimkhan Yandarbiev. Nazarbek is considered the intellectual of the family. "I don't agree. We're condemned to carry on the battle, and the present war is the price we pay for our liberty," he shoots back. The room is silent. Even the nine young children seated on the rug at his feet have fallen quiet as he speaks. "We wanted to build an independent state recognized on the international stage, and it's true that we have failed, but that is due in large part to the Russians," he says. "With the first war everything was destroyed, and we haven't even succeeded in setting up schools for the formation of cadres, the kind of schools that Lenin urged for the creation of the 'new man.' So, yes, the new Chechen man is a total fiasco. As for what's going on today, both sides are to blame: Russia doesn't know what she wants with us, and we ourselves have no idea how to go about achieving this independence of ours. In the end, it's our own people who dragged us into this war. If only we had had another, more progressive government."

Ruslan, the oldest, profits from Nazarbek's brief pause to interrupt him: "If elections were held today in our country, the result could hardly be in doubt. The people would vote for a pro-Russian candidate. There is no other alternative."

To which Nazarbek, the pro-independence civil servant, answers in a dreamy tone, "It's true that this second war is rather strange—more ferocious than the earlier one, though without direct confrontation. The Russian authorities intend to occupy every bit of our territory, and that's just what will happen if nothing changes in Moscow over the next six months. Then, under the occupation, life will get back to normal little by little, until our side, tired of being humiliated, gets the upper hand again. I know exactly what the rebel forces have in their minds. I know them well!"

Suslansbek, the youngest, adds simply, "In any case, we ought to get our independence on paper, which is not yet the case. Only after that can we take concrete steps."

Two rooms away, in the kitchen, where the women are slowly doing the dishes, the dialogue is more down to earth. Zarima chats with her daughter Radima, who is busy cleaning the mud off more than a dozen pairs of shoes.

Radima feels the frustration of any teenager. "I would love it if the Russians occupied Grozny [Zarima raises her eyes heavenward as a sign of her disapproval], because I'm sick to death of the *charia*, tired of not being able to move about freely and of having to wear a scarf."

Zarima casts a sidelong glance in my direction: "Ah, youth."

The young girl adds, a little hesitantly, "I'd also like to see Malik [Saidulayev]* in power. I'm not quite sure why. I read somewhere that he is rich and intelligent."

Her mother brushes her aside. "For the moment, we need one thing only: a little bit of money to buy treats for the children," she says. "Otherwise, life here isn't as terrible as they say. If you sit inside all day long at home at least, nothing will happen to you."

⌒

We're travelling along a stony riverbed that snakes its way between the mountains and descends to the village of Martan Chu in rebel-held territory. A large white flag is flying from the end of a stick mounted on one of the houses. The Russian positions are two kilometers away from these houses and from the little road that climbs up into the fog-shrouded mountain. Our goal is to meet the *boyviki* who have recently left Urus-Martan—considered one of their fiefs—to take refuge in these mountains. We're travelling by tractor. The tractor's enormous tires are equipped with chains for plowing along the bottom of the riverbed. Islam's concern is to find out whether the fighters are Wahhabis or "regulars" he is acquainted with; if the latter, he hopes to persuade them to help us continue our journey. He is afraid that I will end up stuck in a cave somewhere.

---

* Malik Saidulayev is a Chechen billionaire, the inventor of a sort of lottery, whom the Russian authorities would like to install in power in Chechnya.

We roll along for two hours, swerving to avoid clumps of trees or large boulders that have fallen from the high cliffs on either side. As we pass, we catch sight of a few figures descending the slope toward the village, walkie-talkies in hand, mostly unarmed. I spot the stationary silhouette of a young Muslim in an ecstatic pose, palms raised to heaven, praying in this month of Ramadan. The air is filled with the roar of Russian planes. They are an invisible enemy because the cloud cover is unusually low today. Luckily, not one bomb falls.

"Don't be fooled. The Russians know perfectly well who these Wahhabis are and that they're entrenched in these mountains," Makhmud explains. He is a twenty-year-old *boyvik* belonging to an armed faction loyal to President Maskhadov. (He is trying to rejoin his group, and it was at his suggestion that we borrowed his brother's tractor.)

As we approach the "base," Islam immediately realizes that this is not the group he had hoped to find; these are Wahhabis. Nevertheless, he advances toward them through the damp forest. The branches crackle beneath his boots.

They exchange greetings. I hear Islam explain, no doubt, who I am and how the Wahhabis could help us. The emirs* don't usually open their doors to strangers. When he has heard Islam's explanation, one of the chiefs makes his decision: He will allow his men to speak to the "journalist," but he and the other commanders will have "nothing to say," because they are certain that "in any case, the West will never come to our aid." It's not the warmest welcome.

---

* Commanders, in Arabic.

Akhmed Akhmadov is short and stocky. His chest bristles with ammunition. As he talks, he grooms his beard with a comb that he has pulled from his pants pocket. This man is one of the pillars of the mysterious Wahhabi movement. The Chechen people balk at having to live with these "bearded men" who, since the beginning of the 1990s, have been trying to impose their own strict religious laws on the traditional base of Sufi Islam. It's said that the Wahhabis are responsible for most of the kidnappings of Russian and foreign journalists and other visitors to Chechnya. It's also rumored that the Wahhabis are under the control of the commander Khattab.

"We have no ties with anyone, neither Maskhadov, nor Bassayev, nor Khattab," Akhmadov tells Islam laconically. Islam is disappointed; he wants to communicate with one of those three groups in order to rejoin their fighters. "Here in these mountains we are battling the Russians alone," the emir asserts proudly.

From what I can tell, the atmosphere of the camp is not particularly warlike. Base Number 3 is one of fifteen scattered throughout the labyrinthine forest. There are no buildings, only a trailer lightly camouflaged with branches; this can bunk a dozen men. At night, the others stay outdoors; they all take turns sleeping.

I am cold, but no one allows me to draw near to the fire. At last, Islam, who has stayed close to the flames with the leaders, tells me that I can "go warm up in the caravan" with the others. I climb in happily.

Inside, a teenage rebel is kneading bread dough with his shirtsleeves rolled up. There is no woman to do the cooking, and there are few signs of food. The troops strictly observe Ramadam, and eat only at dusk, around 4:30 in the afternoon. They offer me nothing at all, not even hot tea. Ten other mujahedeen, including a Saudi who knows only a few words of Russian, are lounging on a stack of mattresses. One of them is taking a nap. I sit cross-legged in their midst, taking care not to let my trousers show under my long black skirt.

Jars of canned tomatoes and cucumbers stand stacked in a corner. They're parting gifts, no doubt, from mothers and grandmothers who watched as their young sons set off for the forest. Kalachnikovs are hung neatly on the partition, each one on its owner's nail. Videocassettes of the pilgrimage to Mecca are lying about on the windowsill. "We don't have a VCR to view them," the young bread maker comments, "but it's good just to have them." A textbook introduction to Islam in Russian and Arabic circulates among the fighters.

"The Russians send their planes over just at the moment when we're praying," a rebel named Umar explains. "But if they think for a minute that that's going to prevent us from praying to Allah, then they're wrong. We don't stop praying for anything! Like the others here, I've made a pact with Allah: I give Him my body and my life, and He promises me paradise."

Apart from praying, the fighters don't do much. They wait. For what? "For the war to begin," one of them, seated to my right, suggests provocatively. His bright eyes peek out from under an Adidas cap, and his long thin fingers stroke his reddish beard constantly. "It will be a guerilla war that won't stop at our borders. We'll take it onto enemy territory, if necessary, maybe even as far as Moscow. At Urus-Martan we could have held out much longer, at least three months, but they were killing our wives and parents and children with their artillery. It was to put an end to that butchery that we left for the hills, not to please them!"

The redhead, whose name is Luralli, plunges into a long disquisition—propaganda at its most simplistic—on the nature of Wahhabism. "Wahhabis respect the purity of Islam as it was taught by the prophets. That's called Fundamentalism," he exclaims proudly. "We honor that which hasn't been soiled through modernity and the evolution of society."

Although I would like to interrupt him, I listen without saying a word. To get these *boyviki* of my generation to talk—these young men who are suspicious of me but curious at the same time—I have to assume a humble demeanor and ask only the most naïve questions.

"If our own people [the remainder of the Chechen population] don't understand us," he continues, "it's because we have all been educated under the Soviet system, and we desperately lack information on the true Islam. We are here to spread this information." The others look impressed; they listen in silence.

"As for the West"—I have the faint impression that all eyes have shifted to my direction—"they help the Russians. Everybody knows that. I lived in Russia for twelve years, and I know very well that the Russian government doesn't have the means to pay its people. We know perfectly well that the money for the war comes from the West. We're not completely half-witted," he remarks.

Some of the others put in their two cents' worth, but Luralli hasn't much more to say. On the subject of the accusations of kidnapping by the Wahhabis, he offers the same formulaic excuses, putting the blame principally on "Russia, for poisoning the West with this kind of false information." None of them dares to admit that Akhmed Akhmadov has been personally implicated in what has become, in the course of the last three years, a veritable business.

After an hour and a half, Islam, looking worried, opens the door of the trailer and informs me that it's time to leave. We set off once more on the tractor, this time following the riverbed downhill.

"I don't really understand these Wahhabis," Makhmud grumbles. The young rebel has decided to leave the mountains and continue on with us. "If they were really fighting on our side, they would have helped me!"

I ask Islam what he was talking about all that time with the emirs. "About you," he answers briefly. I don't understand at first what he means and ask him to be more explicit. "We sat down by the fire, and they demanded that I give them information about you, the papers you represent, etc. Then, four times, two of them suggested that I simply leave you behind. 'What for?' I asked. 'Cooking, for example. We don't have a woman in the camp.' 'She doesn't know anything about cooking,' I told them."

I laugh at Islam's response, which is exactly what I would have said myself. But I am chilled by the thought of this "polite kidnapping," which I have narrowly escaped. As on all our travels, with the exception of our first two trips, Islam is carrying no weapons, as I requested. We are just two civilians on the move. As a result, Islam's only defense against armed men is the threat of his *tiep*. If these men had attacked me, they would have to answer to Islam and to Islam's entire clan. Before letting us go, the Wahhabis no doubt weighed the consequences of the act they were contemplating. Fortunately, the losses outweighed the gains.

Islam doesn't relax until we get out of the mountains and arrive at Makhmud's family farm. As they serve me, the women of the house—one in fuchsia, the other in yellow—explain that they've always been afraid of those "Wahhabis of Dzhamaat," and that they're happy knowing that they've gone off into the backcountry. I ingest an enormous quantity of soup and tea and slices of warm bread while the others fast.

⌂

The territory of the Republic of Chechnya is divided into villages "where they shoot" and villages "where they don't shoot." Coming from Ingushetia in the direction of the capital, Grozny, one crosses the Russian positions many times. These are not, however, positions in the strict sense of the word, but rather areas within reach of Russian artillery. In the village of Alkhazurovo, where the *zachistka** has not yet begun, it is still possible to find *boyviki* or their supporters operating undercover.

Umar is a doctor. He is also the coordinator of the movements of rebel troops passing through the village to rejoin other bases to the south; he directs the activities of Magomed, a forester by training, who has been promoted to "smuggler of rebel troops" by Khamzat Gulyayev, commander-in-chief of the southwest front.

---

* "Cleansing," that is, verification by the Russian troops of the identity of all the inhabitants of the village, often after a bombardment.

After noting certain recommendations from the doctor, we prepare to set off. It's about a two hour walk to the village of Kordon,
also called Komsomolskoye,* the site of a Pioneer camp.†

The buzzing of Russian helicopters and reconnaissance planes
and the sounds of combat accompany us during our eight-kilome-
ter walk through the damp forest. If I were to surrender to nostal-
gia, the woods would bring back one of my happiest childhood
memories. My parents used to take my brother and me for long
hikes in the country; we would get up early and hike single file
along mountain paths, rarely saying a word until, thrilled and
exhausted, we reached the summit. Here, Magomed is walking in
the lead; he stops often to "listen to" the silence and decide which
path to take. This time, in addition to Islam and me, he's taking
along Musli, a rebel fighter who wants to rejoin his family in
Grozny but who doesn't know the region well. I can't be certain of
what awaits us on the other side. I wonder why the helicopters flying over us are not firing.

As the first houses of Kordon become visible, Magomed signals
anxiously for us to step up the pace. We've scarcely descended the
slope towards the fields when an enormous noise of clashing metal
fills the air. I've been lagging behind the column to examine the
Pioneer camp—which bears the pretty name of "Mountain Air"—
imagining the simple and pleasant life of this vacation colony
under the Soviet Union. I just have time to see Islam ten meters

---

* A locality that was entirely destroyed by the Russians during the last two weeks
  of March 2000.
† The Young Pioneers was a communist youth organization, which indoctrinated
  children aged ten to fourteen throughout the Soviet Union.

ahead of me, his face distorted by a shout that I cannot hear. He's gesturing wildly. I understand that I am to throw myself down on the ground. My face is pressed against the flaccid, muddy earth. Everything trembles as a rain of biting metal pours down upon the countryside. The air has suddenly become very hot. But I am unscathed. I'm alive. I jump up and run toward the group, which has taken shelter among a pile of concrete slabs. The attack is over in less than ten seconds.

The artillery fire is precise. The shells fall less than twenty meters from us. Magomed and Musli are crawling on their knees. They try to wiggle between the slabs, but then crawl out, having no doubt realized that they may get stuck if there's a closer strike. Meanwhile, I stay squatted near Islam, who remains calm. He keeps glancing behind us, where everything is burning. I haven't the courage to look. Islam cradles my head. He wants me to lie on the ground, but I refuse and remain in the same position. I feel as though I no longer exist, and yet all my senses are alert. I tell myself, "I'm going to become deaf, or perhaps I am already." How much longer are they going to fire? I can hardly believe that we are the Russians' targets.

During the rare moments of silence, Islam thinks aloud. "Someone, right here in the village, saw us coming out of the forest and must have radioed our position," he says. "They're shooting back into the woods, where we came from. We mustn't move. They're raking the terrain in a grid pattern, one rectangle after another. Next time it will be there, just in front."

Just once I look behind me to see the picture that corresponds to this horrific noise. Brown earth sprays up several meters high, mingling with metal shards and enormous tongues of orange flame.

There are ten volleys, roughly one every two minutes. After twenty minutes, the air starts to clear. When three minutes of quiet pass, we understand that the shelling is over. None of us has a scratch. Magomed goes first. He starts off at a run, keeping close to a hedge but otherwise he's in the open. A moment later, Islam urges me to follow. I hesitate a fraction of a second: "And you?" "I'm coming right away," he answers. I lift up my black skirt and run through the high weeds, counting (I don't know why) the trunks of the trees I pass in my flight. Some three hundred meters further on, paved road. And suddenly the four of us are walking along the highway, as if nothing had happened.

The 3,000 residents of Kordon have been hidden away in their cellars for ten days or so. No one lives above ground anymore, which gives the erroneous impression that the town is deserted. We stop at the house of the smuggler's nephew to warm ourselves and raise our spirits. In the courtyard, a dozen white sheets are hanging on a clothesline, stiff with ice. "That's so they [the Russians] will realize that people live here and that we're against the war," explains Aminat, one of the four daughters in the family. She shows me the way down to the cellar. The air is stale. Twenty people are living in about fifty square feet of dank, dark space. Four generations, including five young children, are cramped together in this underground hideaway. I sit down on a block of wood, realizing as I do so that I have no strength left. I can scarcely hold the pen to write.

A gasoline lamp burns in a corner. There is no window, and the

flame threatens to flicker out with the explosion of each shell. The
artillery fire has begun again. The two oldest women are invalids.
They pass their time sitting or lying on hard beds made of rugs
spread over wooden planks. Here, too, they carry out their five
*lamaz** every day.

We stay shut up here. Khalifat, the oldest daughter, whose
angular features are highlighted in the pale light of day each time
the door opens, explains the situation. "If you believe the rumors,
there are negotiations going on between the Russians and the
three surrounding villages," she says. "But we can't be sure of it,
and there's no one officially in charge. The Russians always say the
same thing. They want us to chase the *boyviki* out, but how could
we do that? Even if we tell them to get out, they don't listen to us!"

Khalifat spends a lot of time listening to the radio, but she
"doesn't believe a word of what the Russians say." She prefers to
tune in to Radio Svoboda.[†] One of their reporters, Andrei Babitsky, is one of the rare Russian journalists who covers the war from
the Chechen side.[‡] "Yesterday they said that Grozny would fall in
ten days' time. They might just as well kill all of us right now. This
waiting is unbearable!" she moans.

---

* Prayers, in Chechen.

† Russian-language station financed by the United States Senate.

‡ Andrei Babitsky gave highly graphic accounts of the horrors of the war in
Chechnya from behind rebel lines. Frustrated by his "unpatriotic" journalism
and his coverage of Russian atrocities, the Russian government arrested him in
February 2000 and then handed him over to the Chechen rebels, allegedly in
exchange for several Russian POWs. Babitsky reported that in fact he had
been handed over to pro-Moscow Chechens working for the Russian army.
Babitsky was released in March 2000 under pledge not to leave Moscow pend-
ing investigation.

Khalifat has a great deal of trouble feeding the family. When commerce on the public roads became too dangerous, the market in Kordon closed. Her younger sisters, Animat and Lida, are the only ones who make the trip from the cellar to the kitchen in the house. They sprint the forty meters.

"It's not very practical," Animat concedes with a laugh. "Yesterday I burned the meat, and it was all my fault that we had nothing to eat! But how can I know if something's done, when I can't even check the oven because of the bombing?"

Kordon and other villages in the area are supplied by Grozny, Urus-Martan, Shaly, and Shatoy, but the Russian troops have cut all ties between the towns. How do they live when no one can buy food? "Fortunately, we had a supply of flour," Khalifat answers, "and we decided to kill our cow. But in any case we don't have enough for more than two, or maybe three, weeks. And we're lucky that we're in the month of Ramadan! We save a lot that way! We older ones, we try not to eat so much so that the children will have enough."

The family has had enough of this life deep in a cellar, where everything could explode at any moment. Today, when there appears to be a brief respite from the Russian bombardment, the grandfather decides to take half his family to "someplace safe." But where? He would like to go a dozen kilometers to the east, to the hamlet of Starye Atagi, where the Russians have begun talks with the "village elders." One of the nephews, Riamzan, has looked into the possibility of finding lodging there. Having no relatives in the area, they set out blindly. As night falls, the nineteen members of the family pile into the back of Riamzan's dump truck, sur-

rounded by mattresses, rugs, an iron bedstead, and sacks of provi-
sions. We decide to leave with them.

The Russians have destroyed the most traveled bridge, so we
will have to cross the Argun River twice. We must also give thanks
to Allah for not coming under a bombardment during this trip,
which seems interminable. I am squeezed between heavy bundles
of cloth and a piece of ironwork that presses against my legs. Islam
tries to protect me from the wind with a piece of carpet. As we
ride along, the four girls pass their time reminiscing about their
childhood. I hear the accents of their voices, babbling in a kind of
universal little-girl talk. "You remember, the time I pushed you off
the top of the slide. You were knocked out a couple of minutes,
and the whole village thought it was the end," Aminat says to
Lida. "And how!" Lida answers. "Those were the good old days.
We hadn't the faintest notion of war."

∩

At last we arrive at Starye Atagi, fief of the former pro-independence president Zelimkhan Yandarbiev. The small town of 11,000
inhabitants surrendered to Federal forces, after the usual ritual, on
December 5, 1999. The "elders" took part in talks with the Russians, who promised not to target the small agglomeration. But, if
we are to believe numerous reports and the all-night rumbling of
artillery, the Russians are continuing their fire. The Federals will
eventually institute a "passport régime" that will allow them to
verify everyone's identity, including the houses on their blacklist.
But they haven't begun yet. "It's because they don't have enough

men," explains Khassan, a former agronomist on a Soviet state farm. "The army can't take charge of it because it belongs by rights to the Interior. As usual, there's not a lot of cooperation between the two of them," he adds.

It was at Novye Atagi, on the other side of the bridge over the Argun River, that four Red Cross doctors were savagely murdered in 1996. Most of the nongovernmental organizations left Chechnya as a consequence of that killing. On this side of the bridge, at the Starye Atagi hospital, they remember the events very well and regret them to this day.

"Since then we've had no help at all, and that's to be expected," says Khamzat, a thirty-five-year-old surgeon. "But they can't just leave us in this condition, with no means at all to treat the casualties of this war."

Khamzat belongs to a team of six doctors, all from Grozny; they staff the surgical unit in this hospital, which serves the three central regions of Chechnya, including the capital. Of the hospital's four floors, only one is equipped to receive the sick and the wounded. The ground floor is "undergoing repairs," and two other floors have suffered bomb damage. When we enter, we must take off our shoes; it's the only way to conserve even a semblance of cleanliness in the building. In a corner, twenty stretchers lean against the wall. The electricity functions thanks to a generator that is constantly blowing fuses. Most of the injured are victims of artillery fire; they suffer wounds to the head, fractures, and burns from shell bursts. As elsewhere in the region, most of patients buy their medicines on the open market, and if their families do not have the means to supply anesthesia, they go without. The same goes for food, because the doctors are unable to organize a meal service. Sometimes the women of the village bring in a pot of soup or a piece of cooked meat, which is shared equitably among those patients who need it most.

Ima, a twenty-two-year-old patient is lying in bed under a thin blanket topped with a pile of coats. There has been no heat since the first days of the conflict. "I wanted to flee to the Ingushetia border," she recounts. "We were walking west, my husband and I and some others, on the road toward Goyty. Suddenly, without any warning, they fired on us. I was wounded in the chest, the leg, and the shoulder. I don't even know who brought me here."

Leila, her mother, is extremely grateful to the surgeons, who not only saved Ima's life but sent someone to search for her family: "Someone came to my house four days after the disaster to tell me that Ima was in the hospital at Starye Atagi. I couldn't believe it. I was sure she was dead because her husband had told me that he couldn't find her after the attack and that there were many bodies that were impossible to identify."

Ima's mother keeps a handkerchief pressed to her breast. She sometimes gazes at its contents, as if they were precious relics. "These are the bits of shrapnel that almost killed my daughter," she explains. "The doctors removed them from her body. It's a miracle that she can walk."

Eight men, ranging in age from sixteen to fifty-four, fill the beds on the second-floor ward. Out of the eight, three are amputees. One of them, a young man, cries out to me, "Russia can go right on firing on us, we're not afraid of them! We fear only Allah!"

I wake up the next morning in a house in Starye Atagi. We arrived here yesterday evening after a long and difficult trip by truck, followed by many kilometers on foot. Along the way, we had to cross a wooden suspension bridge over the icy Argun River. As I shuffled across in the fading light, I felt sure I would slip and disappear forever into swirling waters below.

We're staying with family friends of Musli, the rebel fighter. I am sleeping in the old double bed belonging to the parents, whose room has been transformed into "women's quarters"; even during Ramadan and wartime, family or not, men and women are segregated into separate parts of the house.

Laulli, the patriarch, is a large fellow with a bushy mustache. His family consists of his wife, who is small and discreet, their older son, his wife, their baby of three months, and their second daughter, Amina, who is as yet unmarried. Their other daughter, Teresa, reminds me of Magomed's daughter in Achkhoy-Martan, who confided to me the misery of her marriage to a man she detests. The situation in this family is almost identical: Teresa has a seven-year-old son from a first marriage, a three-year-old son from her present husband, whom she abhors—he lives in the house across the road—and she's pregnant with a third child. This makes many mouths to feed every day, without counting guests such as us.

As Laulli explains to me, the towns under Russian control, like this one, serve as rest stops for the *boyviki*, who stay for a few days at a time, touch base with their families, catch up on their sleep without the fear of bombs, and replenish their food supplies. Although it's difficult and dangerous to go from place to place—the safest form of travel is still by foot—everybody is on the move, especially the men.

᠕

The bent old woman is repacking her plastic bags with winter clothing and wool socks, which she had spread out on a square of fabric on top of the dried mud early this morning. It's barely three in the afternoon, and already a rumor is making the rounds that the Russians have imposed a local curfew—called, in its literal translation, the "commander's hour."

"No, no, this is all fantasy!" Anzor Dhivrolibov assures us. Anzor is a resident of Novye Atagi and has been a local parliamentary deputy since 1997. "There isn't any curfew here, and there never will be. That's only lies. It just goes to show how frightened everyone is, that's all," he thunders, his face crimson.

Anzor is much more than a deputy. He has been known as the "White Wolf" since the days of the Soviet Union, when he was in charge of stock at the huge regional cement factory. "I stayed there until 1995," he tells me. He is comfortably ensconced in a deep faux-antique armchair in the "male" wing of his living room. "Until the first war, when the Russians completely destroyed the factory. What to do? I didn't search long for an answer. I gave much of the money that I had put aside to the rebels. It was my way of helping them, because physically, I wasn't able to take up arms. Later we had elections, and many people encouraged me to run."

Two days before, fifteen or so soldiers invaded Anzor's vast residence—where he lives with his wife, his three daughters, and his sister-in-law and her son, all refugees from Grozny, as well as fifteen other refugees—to carry out the usual identity checks.

"They even checked the titles of the films on our videocassettes," Elena, Anzor's wife complains, and adds, "I understand that they would be drawn to a house like ours, thinking that there would be something here they could take. Praise God, when they came up against my husband, they didn't dare touch a thing!"

Anzor represents real authority. During the first war, his imposing red-brick home was the site of hundreds of hours of talks between the rebel commander of the period, Aslan Maskhadov, and Russian officials. "I have in my possession an archive of videocassettes. I'm probably the only one who has viewed every one of them," the master of the house explains. "And here, as well, I received many mothers of Russian soldiers, when we were having the prisoner exchanges. Everything took place in this room."

Anzor has only one regret: That the accords of Khasavyiurt are not known instead as the "accords of Novye Atagi." "All the preparation for this agreement took place in my house," he recalls with emotion, "and General Alexander Lebed* and Aslan Maskhadov had a rendezvous right here, on a Thursday, to sign it. But two days

---

* Presently governor of the region of Krasnoyarsk in Siberia. At the time, he was appointed by President Yeltsin to conduct the peace talks in Chechnya.

before, some imbeciles from the Chechen side stole fifty Kalachnikovs from a Russian camp. Lebed ordered them to return them
immediately and threatened to postpone the signing. They wouldn't
give them back, so the treaty was signed later, at Khasavyurt!"

Anzor knows the Russian generals well because he often
"exchanged cement for soldiers," he delights in recalling. "But this
time," he adds, "I'm afraid that we won't see negotiations anytime
soon. What advantage would they have for Russia? We'll have to
wait until after the presidential elections."

While waiting, Anzor remains active. At the risk of his life, he
carried on discussions with Shamanov's troops, who had surrounded Novye Atagi and Chiri Yurt: "No one would agree to go
and meet with them. Meanwhile, there were more and more losses
in the civilian population of our town. I got in my Volga and
drove up to the top of the hill where they were camping, so they
could see me clearly. There wasn't a road. I had to go on foot,
under artillery fire. At the last house in the village, I asked for a
piece of white material, which I attached to a stick. I came down
the slope waving my flag. I knew they had seen me because they
were firing all around me but not right at me. Even so, they never
stopped firing. When I got within earshot, I shouted, 'Comrades,
could you stop for just a moment?' They were rather surprised to
see a deputy put his life on the line like that."

The artillery is no longer firing on Novye Atagi; it's now tar-
geting the road to Grozny.

Adam Atsupov, a deputy from the district of Grozny, has
found temporary shelter with Anzor. This mustachioed former
engineer-economist, whose front teeth are all capped with gold,

chimes in with his own story. "I was in Grozny four days ago. It's hell there, and there are many people left. The cellars are full. The worst thing is the lack of water. For heat, they're burning anything they can find, even sawing down the electricity poles. They'll take Grozny, there's no doubt about it. We have almost no weapons—a few Stingers we got from Afghanistan, some Igla antiaircraft batteries, the oldest ones in the Soviet arsenal. The hardest part is getting out of town. We attempted it in a three-car convoy. Fortunately, I was traveling in the last one, because the Russians set their sights on the two ahead of me. I just had time to throw myself out of the car. I continued on foot."

Unlike Anzor, Adam's wife and children are in Ingushetia. "This war will last a long time," Adam predicts as he adds wood to the stove. "Over the last three years we've tried hard to win recognition from international organizations such as the Council of Europe. We've been to Iceland, because they were the first country to recognize the three Baltic states. It was in vain. Now we find ourselves alone in the world, between the hammer and the sickle!" According to Adam, the Wahhabis are the great culprits: "We want a modern state with traditional Islam, but these Wahhabis work against us, and they foment trouble. They're the ones who recruit and train our young people and put guns in their hands!"

Once a week, when there is a quorum, the parliament meets to discuss the situation. "But it's difficult to find a meeting place that is convenient for all of us," Adam explains. "We have decided that for important questions, such as the status of our republic, the signature of the president of the parliament, Ruslan Alikhadzhiev, will be enough to authenticate documents."

The most recent meeting of the thirty-two deputies took place in Shaly, and Adam isn't sure yet where the next one will occur. In the meantime, he circulates with the rest of his colleagues among the front lines, compiling information on the needs of the forces and trying to find solutions. According to Adam, a third of the Chechen parliamentary deputies have become battalion commanders.

Adam gets up from his chair and asks me to follow him outdoors because he wants to show me something. We walk the distance from the large brick residence to the town cemetery, which is large but well tended. In front of the entrance, Adam stops for a moment. "How many innocent victims die every day!" he exclaims. According to tradition, each grave is a simple mound of earth with a tall rectangular stone inscribed in Arabic. On more than fifty of these graves the earth is fresh.

Mumadi Saidayev, in civilian dress—a maroon suit and sweater, no tie—stops for a moment to talk with me. His car is parked under a tree in open country twenty or thirty kilometers from Grozny. This ruddy man with a hard and sometimes bitter look in his eyes is the Chechen Chief of the General Staff, the number two man after President Aslan Maskhadov. He's in charge of military strategy. Against the blackness of the night, an orange fire emanates from the southern suburbs of the capital, lighting up the sky. The Russians are sweeping over the residential areas and releasing their bombs. From afar, the murderous spectacle looks grandiose.

"First," begins Mamudi, "you mustn't attach too much importance to the Russian attacks on Grozny. There have been lots of
them, it's true, and even last week, there was the column of tanks
that advanced into the center of the city, as far as Minutka Square.
The Russians move forward methodically, little by little. But from
the beginning of this offensive, they haven't been able to maintain
their advances. They thought they would arrive in Grozny within
three days, but the fighting lasted more than a month in the
northern territories. The Russians will take Grozny—or at least
they'll try. That's to be expected. Now that they've come this far,
they'll want to go farther," he explains coldly, in a monotone. This
former Soviet officer, an intelligence specialist, is familiar with the
strategy of his enemies.

Mumadi, who has spent most of his life in Latvia with the Red
Army, was wounded three times in the preceding war. He still carries a piece of shrapnel in his knee. It has left him with a limp.

"It's always the same scenario," he says. They send their scouts
out, and if they run into some resistance, they beat a hasty retreat
and begin shelling. At the moment, they're firing ground-to-ground
missiles from a distance of ninety kilometers, as well as Scuds, which
—like the Hurricane and Grad missiles—have been outlawed for use
against residential areas by international conventions."

Throughout our conversation, Mumadi stops to gulp down
long drafts of mineral water. He seems unable to quench his thirst.
He also refuses to admit that the rebel forces are growing weaker.
Although the Russian troops appear to be advancing steadily, this
man, who was president of the Central Electoral Commission for
the general election of January 1997, appears serenely confident.

"Just because the Russian troops occupy territory, it doesn't mean that they're gaining in influence," Mumadi explains. His walkie-talkie squawks continuously in the background. "In fact, they'll control only what is inside the perimeter of their checkpoints, while the rest of the territory will be in the hands of the guerillas; that is, us. If the Russians spread out geographically, it will be harder for them to communicate. That will be the moment for us to act. With little groups of five men we'll be able to ambush entire columns."

Mumadi Saidayev deplores not only the heavy civilian losses, but also the ecological damage. "Since we've been without water and gas since the month of August," he says, "people have begun to cut down the woodlands, which has been a great shock to the ecosystem. All sorts of polluting debris has fallen into the Sunzha River, which runs into the Caspian Sea. Nature is feeling the effects of this cataclysm, and it will go well beyond our frontiers. They'll be harvesting tainted fruit for several generations. But who here worries about the future?" he asks, shrugging his shoulders and taking another gulp of mineral water.

Communication also preoccupies the head of the Chechen General Staff. The only means of communicating among the various groups of *boyviki* is by radio. "The Russians can listen in on us all the time, and that gives them a definite advantage. We can't do the same to them for lack of equipment. Of course, we speak in code, and never for very long at a time; and then, too, we're always changing our positions, but they pick up everything. It's a problem. For instance, we try to avoid mentioning our losses."

In Chechnya, where, for the second time in less than ten years, they're fighting for their independence—"not to steal territory that doesn't belong to us, but to preserve the right to live on our own," as Mumadi Saidayev puts it—the current Russian legislative elections elicit no reaction from the population.* Even the presidential contest, which is due to happen in six months, interests no one: "Nothing will change with a new president. On the contrary, things could even be worse, for instance, if Vladimir Putin were elected. The ones who started this war simply cannot not pursue it to the very end. That would be political suicide."

For Mumadi, the only date that matters is the next monthly meeting of the GKP, the State Defense Committee, which brings together President Maskhadov and the six commanders in charge of the Chechen fronts.

The ex-Soviet officer has only one regret: That Russian public opinion is now behind its leaders. Will there be negotiations? "No question of it, at least not before the elections. For the ordinary Russian, taking revenge against the Chechens is a dream come true. As a matter of fact, this is the goal of the LDPR,† the party of the extreme right. After the elections they'll surely change their minds, because they'll need to work toward some kind of compromise. The military will, in any case, do what Putin orders them to do. They're soldiers. They obey their superiors, and, therefore,

---

* These elections took place on December 19, 1999. In contrast with the presidential vote of March 26, 2000, they were not organized on Chechen territory.
† A right-wing party directed by the ultranationalist Vladimir Jirinovsky.

their president. As soon as the Russian government feels they're nearing victory, as soon as they have satisfied, even a little bit, their imperialist urge, they won't be afraid of talks any longer."

Then Mumadi adds, with great self-confidence, "You wouldn't need much to turn their public opinion around. For example, if we struck a hard blow at one of their elite divisions, from Moscow or the area around it. Then they'd see how easy it is to die in Chechnya!"

Chapter 6

"MY GREATEST HOPE is that this war will end and that everyone will live together normally again," Tamara announces, choosing her words carefully. As she speaks, she rocks back and forth on the bed that passes for a sofa in one of the bedrooms of her house. I'm in Sleptsovskii, only a few meters from the Chechen border.

An ample woman with sparkling light gray eyes and a face wrinkled by years of worry and hard work, Tamara is the mother of eight children, six boys and two girls. Before the war, her life was peaceful, dominated by the rhythm of her pregnancies. She lived according to the ancestral traditions of her people. Like others before her, she nursed her infants, raised them to adulthood, married them off, and bought houses for each of her sons. She is proud of her life and of her offspring, even if now, after two wars, she senses the gaps in their education: "I raised them all with a simple philosophy: Respect others so that you'll be respected your-self; be kind to everyone so that no one may speak ill of you; honor your elders and listen patiently to those who are younger. Unfortunately, they've grown up at the very worst time. They don't want to get married, don't know where to go or what to do. It's as if they had no future. All my life I've talked to them about respect for their fellow man. After all, that's what makes us human, isn't it?"

Tamara sighs. She stretches her legs, which are cramped from sitting too long in the same position, and rearranges herself cross-legged. She pushes back the multicolored headscarf around her abundant gray hair. Then she raises her big thoughtful eyes to me and asks "if the questions are almost over." She's sure that what she has to say won't interest anybody. I urge her to continue.

"And then this war came along and ruined everything," she sighs. "People today are losing their minds. They've had to leave their homes; they've lost everything. Before the war, I was calm and happy. Living was no problem. It's the war that's the problem!"

Fortunately, Tamara hasn't had to leave her large house, crowded now with her husband and seven of their children, a daughter-in-law and her newborn son, her sister, her eighty-five-year-old mother-in-law, and fifteen refugees.

In 1976, after years of hard manual labor in Siberia, Tamara and her husband, Daud, were able to buy a plot of land that included an old *izbushka*, a simple, Russian-style wooden house. It took them almost ten years to transform the house into a real brick residence with two floors, "the first in the neighborhood," Tamara recalls with pride. For many years their salaries went into the house. With the partition of the Autonomous Soviet Socialist Republic of Checheno-Ingushetia into two entities, their little town of Sleptsovskii, seventy kilometers west of Grozny and thirty kilometers east of Nazran, fell on the Ingush side of the border. "To put it simply, we ended up where the bombs aren't falling," Tamara explains, pleased, although a bit surprised, at her own formulation. "In any case, we Chechens consider this Ingush land as our own. It has always been a mixture of the two peoples."

What about the frontier that is sometimes open, sometimes closed, depending upon the good will of the Russian soldiers?

"They'll have to withdraw, sooner or later," Tamara says. "In 1988, at the beginning of Gorbachev's *perestroika*, we bought four houses at once from Russians who were leaving the Caucasus. Many people bought property at that time. It was a very good deal. Our houses are in the village of Assinovskii, less than ten kilometers from here, in Chechnya. We needed them for our sons because the eldest will remain here in our house, but the five younger ones will need their own homes in which to raise their own families. We need two more, in fact, for the two youngest."

At that time, Tamara's husband had decided not to buy property in Sleptsovskii because there was nothing interesting on the market. Less than six years later, in December 1994, the first Russo-Chechen war broke out, and they had to leave in haste.

"Fortunately, the old *izba* in Sleptsovskii was still there to offer us refuge. We had never for a moment imagined that a real frontier would separate us. We were worried sick," Tamara recalls sadly. "In December, all our stored grain was over there, and we lost everything when we fled in a taxi. Everyone knew that it would be safer on the Ingush side. But what they didn't know was how long it would last, and especially, that this nightmare would start again in the autumn of 1999. Between the two wars, we had an inkling of what was to come, so we didn't go back to live on the Chechen side. Only Riamzan, our second son, returned to settle in one of the houses with his new wife. We had to bring them back here double-quick this fall. I went to fetch them myself in the car. Three days after their arrival here in Sleptsovskii, my daughter-in-law gave birth to a son."

Since then, every two weeks or so, Tamara musters her courage and goes over "to the other side" to check on the state of the four houses. She checks on what's been stolen, what's been damaged, and what's left of their possessions. "The doors are wide open, the locks are forced, and people help themselves to what's there," she explains. On occasion, refugees spend several nights but take nothing. "They're not all vandals. When it comes down to it, I'd rather have refugees than Russians," she adds softly.

Tamara knows the Russians well, and her feelings about them are mixed. Her first impressions of Russians were formed during her period of exile in Kazakhstan. She was exiled at the age of two, the youngest in a family of nine children: "My oldest sister took care of us while our parents worked on the collective farm. We didn't have the right to leave the village. We buried our grandfather there."

Although she was still a young child, she remembers the train trip back to her native country quite clearly: "We got out in the town of Samashkii and stayed with friends. There was a big celebration because everyone was coming home [from exile]. They slaughtered a sheep for us. I remember that we were supposed to stay a week. In the end, we lived there two years."

The real homecoming took place when the family decided to return to their ancestral land, in the mountain village of Arshty, now in Ingushetia. "All the men in the family got busy building houses on our old land. The houses were made of wood, not brick, but my father was as proud as a pope. You'd think he was building Moscow! And I was at long last reunited with my *rod*, the clan my father had told me so much about."

The adolescent Tamara learned Russian at school in Arshty. At home they spoke Chechen. "Our teacher was a Russian woman, Vera Fedorovna. In fact, she lived just like us. She was married to a Chechen."

In 1961, Tamara's father fell ill and died. Tamara lived with her mother until her marriage, eight years later: "I met Daud, my future husband, down on the plain in Sleptsovskii. He noticed me as I was getting off a bus on my way to my sewing lessons. He came to call. Three months later, I packed my suitcase and left with him without a word to my mother. We didn't talk much about those things then. I was happy because down on the plain, they had gas, which wasn't available in Arshty, and still isn't today."

With the beginning of her married life came motherhood. In twelve years Tamara would give birth nine times. "In those days there was no abortion," Tamara says carefully.

But soon the small Caucasian Republic of Checheno-Ingushetia, where the *khozyain*,* her husband, worked instructing

---

* Master of the house, in Russian.

truck drivers, could no longer meet the demands of the growing family. They would need to find work elsewhere, in the vast Soviet Union. "We looked for special assignments," Tamara recalls. "Daud became a mason, then a foreman. I joined him as soon as I stopped nursing the babies. We took the big children with us and left the little ones with their grandmother. In the Soviet Union, I cooked or helped out with construction jobs on garages and stables. And in October we came back here for the winter."

Tamara describes this time as one of the happiest in her life. "We loved Siberia in particular. The things we built there! My *khozyain* was in charge of a team. He was good at finding the raw materials they needed. We put all our energy into that work. Of course, for the Russians, we were always Chechens, but we gave as good as we got, and in the end we managed to live together quite comfortably. We didn't eat in the canteen with the Russians; we made our own meals, separately. We've even kept some friends there from that time. We used to hear from them—until last October. Nothing since. No doubt it's because of this second war," she sighs.

＾

Sleptsovskii doesn't agree with Islam. He has changed suddenly and has plunged into a deep depression. One evening he describes his mental state, mixing up in his jumbled flow of words a description of his symptoms and the expression of his feelings, which is rare for him. He is obsessed with the memory of one of his best friends, who died in 1996 in Bamut.

"He was so beautiful, beautiful like a woman!" Islam says. "He always said that when he was with me he wasn't afraid of dying. And he died without me. We weren't together that day. On that evening—it was August 6 [1996]—I was in Grozny for the counteroffensive, and he had stayed in Bamut. When I learned of his death, big tears like pearls began to run down my cheeks. I never knew I could cry like that. I started out right away for Bamut.* As the sun was rising, I was almost there, and I arrived just in time for his burial. I'm talking about it to you today because it's my duty to remember him. There's no one else who remembers. He didn't have a wife or a child. He doesn't exist any longer. While I—I'm still living."

It's evening. Islam tells me that he wants to go to sleep and not wake up until "it's all over." I understand that feeling. Islam can no longer bear these comings and goings between Chechnya, his own mutilated country where every hamlet recalls the death of a friend, and Ingushetia, where everyone, including his family, is in turmoil. There is no life and no home for him anywhere. His nerves are shot. He doesn't drink, doesn't smoke, but he chews constantly on sunflower seeds. It's a nervous habit; he slips one seed after another into his mouth and chews mechanically, his head bowed, without a word.

⌒

At the end of a long dirt road strewn with trees felled by the violent winds, we come upon some fifteen multicolored tents. Their

---

* About sixty kilometers from Grozny.

colors are faded, but they are surrounded by a playground, a soccer field, and an orchard. This is the temporary home of fifty-six children, all orphans, all Chechens from Grozny. Islam waits for me in the car; he doesn't want to see the orphans.

"In early September, when this second war seemed to me inevitable, I said to myself that we must find a place where the children could go on living without the danger of bombings," explains Aslambek Dombayev. The director of Grozny's central orphanage "in exile" is speaking to me from his bed because he is suffering from a nasty bout of flu. "In fact, when the planes began to fly over us, the children begged to go," he adds, putting on his glasses.

Rosa, his wife and colleague of thirty years, explains, "During the previous war we also had to be evacuated. Our orphanage is right in the center of Grozny, and we were sure we would be bombed." The orphans were moved to villages far from the capital. "Today, it's not even worth thinking about. The war has infiltrated into the most remote corners of our republic."

Aslambek seems eager to talk about his own Soviet past: "At the time, our goal was to create a new kind of shelter where the family would be re-created and not destroyed. The older children would look after the younger ones. We were preparing the children for their entry into society with the help of teachers, professors, and even artists. We had about 450 children in our care."

His wife continues, "At the end of the Soviet Union, when new forces emerged, everyone grabbed onto the idea of independence. But it was like a motor that sputters and dies. We couldn't function any longer without sponsors, and I spent my time trying to raise money." With the outbreak of the first war, Chechnya produced more and more orphans. "But we couldn't take all of them in," Rosa laments, "because we had to have legal proof of the death of the parents, along with a hundred other administrative documents."

On September 28, 1999, everyone piled into a bus for Ingushetia. Before that, Aslambek had asked the authorities of the pro-independence government for permission to evacuate the fifty-six orphans, all between three and seventeen years old. "President Maskhadov agreed immediately," the director recalls. "He himself suggested Ingushetia and even gave me a letter to carry to Ruslan Auchev. Auchev was extraordinary. He literally made us a gift of this place."

A year earlier, the Ingush government had created the first "Rehabilitation Center for Underprivileged Children" on this former Soviet Pioneer site. Space was subsequently made available for their "little Chechen brothers." Here, the children receive three meals a day, but they have no hot water, their electricity is regularly cut off, and the orphanage has no toys for the very young.

"Ten of our children have been admitted into the high school at Troitsk, the locality we belong to," says Aslambek proudly. "As for the others, unfortunately no one will take them, and we don't have time to focus on each one individually. So they're a bit at loose ends. But the important thing is that we have them with us and not one of them has perished."

Humanitarian aid, which was available during the first war, is rare this time. "The first to come to our assistance were the Doctors Without Borders, then the Red Cross, and, most recently, a Jewish organization based in Moscow," Rosa points out.

With a surprisingly nimble gesture, Aslambek suddenly raises the mattress of his bed. "Here are our archives!" he says, laughing. In between the wooden slats of the bed are stuffed all the press clippings concerning aid the orphanage has received, as well as yellowed photos of members of the orphanage from different periods.

"Our life before the war," says Rosa with a sigh.

Nearby, in a clean but meagerly decorated dormitory, twelve-year-old Maussa is drawing with felt pens, using photos from a 1967 almanac as models. "These are towers, real towers made of stone, from the village of my ancestors," the child declares gravely. "Today, I'm sure, they don't exist any longer, but I like drawing them anyway."

⌂

The line in front of the old wooden door bearing the sign "Department of Neuropsychiatry, open every day from 8:00 A.M. to 5:00 P.M., except Sundays" is long, extending halfway up the stairs. The patients are a heterogeneous group, about fifteen in all, mostly women. They are all looking down at their feet. The lips of one woman tremble uncontrollably. A few young men are also waiting; they lean against the wall or rest their elbows on the banister and stare expressionlessly into space. From time to time, the blue door opens part way and a tired female voice calls out officiously: "Next!" I walk in. It's a tiny office with two tables. A woman is sitting behind each table. There is also a hospital bed. The walls are grayish, the light harsh. A naked light bulb hangs from the end of a black electric cord.

"Sit down. What brings you here?" asks the nurse, poised over a form she is ready to fill out.

"I am French, a journalist. I would like to talk to you a bit about your work, if you have a moment."

Both women raise their heads and stare at me, astonished.

"But you didn't have to wait in line!" the psychiatrist exclaims. She is amused and also curious.

We arrange to meet at a time when I can come to see her without disturbing her work.

Neyla Kornienko is the psychiatrist on duty this morning. The other woman is a nurse. From morning until night they listen to the problems of a mixed (Russian, Chechen, Ingush) population struggling to survive the deplorable and disorienting conditions of war. Discretely but elegantly made-up, Neyla wears a tall white hat, which makes her look a bit like a chef in a grand restaurant, and a beige wool shawl, which she has thrown over her white blouse to ward off the chill of her office. She is forty-two. She gives her analysis of the situation: "It's very simple. Before the hostilities, the local population lived quietly in the Republic of Checheno-Ingushetia. They lived together. Today, this entity has been cut in two, with the frontier only several kilometers away from here. One side—Chechnya—is fighting, while the other—Ingushetia—receives their refugees and remains passive. It's an immeasurable trauma, from which everyone suffers without exception. I know what I'm talking about. I myself am a refugee from Grozny," she is careful to point out.

Neyla is Russian. But because she is married to a Chechen—from whom she is presently separated—she lives in Grozny, where she worked as a child psychiatrist at Hospital Number 9, until it was destroyed by bombs.

"My patients are astonished to discover that I come from Grozny." Neyla says. "The problem is that very few Russian specialists have chosen to remain in the region. They have all left for Krasnodar, Piatigorsk, and Mineralnye Vody [other cities in the Caucasus], where they feel safer and where they have family."

In 1992, the small territory of Ingushetia hardly had any real infrastructure, including medical. It was only in 1995, when Neyla arrived from Grozny, that the hospital in the small town of Sleptsovskii decided to open a neuropsychiatric service. Her monthly salary amounts to 1,200 rubles ($50).

"The chief problem is that, traditionally, in the Caucasus, it isn't correct to seek help from a "doctor of the soul," as they call us here. But the psychological pressure is so devastating, and the shadow of the war so oppressive, that people have suddenly begun to come in for consultations. But they do everything here "as a family," which poses other problems. Here I am everything at once: Confidante, social worker, purveyor of medications and advice. And all of it is free, of course!"

Often a member of the family, someone who's "sane or who considers himself to be so" presents the case of a brother, father, cousin, husband, or nephew. "But a woman—because it is most often women I see—never comes alone; she is always accompanied by her chaperone," Neyla adds. It is much rarer, but sometimes a man will come alone. "They tell me: I need help. Give me medicine to calm me."

Neyla cites the example of a twenty-five-year-old Chechen who, immediately upon entering her office, announced: "I am psychologically ill. I can't find my place in society!" Neyla was intrigued by such a discerning self-diagnosis, and she listened as the young patient told her how he had survived the first war, how many of his comrades had been killed, how ashamed he was not to have died in their place, and how much he suffers in this second conflict from his lack of "contact" with the Russian forces.

With a horrifying jolt, I suddenly realize that this man, this young, lost twenty-five-year-old, must surely be Islam!

"Of course, we're talking about a combatant, and many of them do come to see me about their anxieties, which are caused directly or indirectly by the war," Neyla continues. "Here, everyone is depressed. And I have almost no medicine to dispense. Patients have to buy it themselves, and it's too expensive." According to Neyla, the Sleptsovskii hospital has only one psychiatric clinic, and it's not a real department with beds. As a result, there's nowhere to keep patients overnight and monitor their medications. "When all is said and done, we're not really sure that we serve a useful purpose," she admits.

For Neyla, who sees fifteen to twenty patients a day, one thing is certain: "Ninety-nine percent of the inhabitants of this former Soviet republic have experienced some kind of trauma." This goes back to the distant past. "In 1991, no one was ready for the end of the Soviet Union and still less for the ascent of a man such as Yeltsin. Then the Baltic countries left the Federation. Here, that produced a great shock. Finally, the Republic of Checheno-

Ingushetia was split in two. The result has been that most of the men exhibit aggressive, even schizophrenic, behavior, and the women often fall into deep depressions."

Today, Neyla has seen two refugees from Achkhoy-Martan who came to get medicine for their epileptic son; a woman from Samashkii seeking a place in a clinic for her schizophrenic husband; and another refugee complaining of persistent headaches. "But most of the time," Neyla emphasizes, "I am overcome by my own inability to deal with the situation. Sometimes, I don't even know what to advise. The patient forgets the cause of his illness. All he wants is to feed his family. He wants a roof over his head and heat within his four walls. How can I help him?"

Just as she is finishing her sentence, at 5:30 P.M., the lights go out, plunging the hospital into darkness.

⌒

We set off once more for Chechnya in a gloomy mood, though Islam seems to have recovered some of his old energy. We pass through the now familiar Kavkaz checkpoint in a minibus bound for Urus-Martan. A dozen other passengers are traveling with us. No problems. The soldiers glance vaguely at our papers, but don't even search our bags. In any case, they would find nothing compromising in mine. Everything is on my person. My camera and notebooks are stuffed into various pants pockets, under my skirt, and in my boots, and my satellite telephone—in a small but cumbersome case—is strapped to my waist, held in place by a scarf.

The landscape I now know so well passes by outside our windows. The trees are sparser, and more and more Russian soldiers are posted along the road with nothing to do. Everywhere children are playing a favorite winter game. They watch for a passing car or truck, then jump behind it and slide a few meters clinging to its bumper, to the great annoyance of the driver. Women are pulling heavy wooden sleds with ropes, hauling fifty-liter milk containers, now used for water. They fetch this water from nearby wells or from the frozen puddles by the side of the road. The air is cold and dry; the sky is a wintry gray. The mountains stand out against the horizon as if someone had delicately positioned them there.

When we arrive at Urus-Martan, we set off on the same path we took the last time to see whether Islam's friends have returned now that the town has been taken.

When we reach the house, we see that the cut wood is now piled under the covered part of the courtyard, out of reach of the snow. Heaps of shoes are lying about the foot of the steps leading to the wooden door, a sure sign that there are people inside. The windows still have no glass, but two layers of plastic sheeting have been carefully attached to the casings.

At the beginning of December, when Urus-Martan was under heavy fire from the Russians, this house stood abandoned. Today, three of the eight Khabdiev brothers have come back with their wives and children. They have all enrolled in the militia of Gantemirov, the former mayor of Grozny. One of them, Said-Mogamed, can't hide his disappointment: "These *gantemirovtsy**

---

* Gantemirov's men, in Russian.

have absolutely no role except to attract public attention. The Russians would like the outside world to think that the Chechens are on their side. Of course, that isn't true. It's just a line; it's publicity!"

Above our heads, the throbbing of helicopters will not cease before nightfall. "They're building a military airport," Said-Mogamed explains. He gets up, changes his clothes, and goes out to do his rounds with thirty other militiamen.

Said-Mogamed is small, dark, and stocky, and is often taken for a Wahhabi. His wife, Lisa, thinks that it's only because he has a mustache and a beard. She is bathing their daughter Maaka in a tin tub. Again and again, she patiently pours water from a cup over the child's shaved head—shaved "so that her hair will grow back more quickly and more beautiful." Mother and child keep close to the wood stove so that Maaka doesn't catch cold. When she has finished her daughter's bath, Lisa washes Maaka's clothes in the bath water while Maaka tries to pull on her patched woolen tights.

"My hands ache," Lisa concedes, once her husband is gone. "All day I have them in water, either boiling hot or ice-cold. All the time I'm cooking and washing, with no break. It's exhausting. I have three children, and I don't want any more. With this war on, it simply isn't possible."

Her two older children, boys aged eight and twelve, have gone to play at their grandmother's, at the other end of the street. Lisa is only twenty-nine, but she speaks of the past as if she were already an old woman. "Before Dudayev came to power, we went to the province of Stavropol every summer," she says. "We stayed at

Soviet Farm Number 9 to grow watermelons. Then we sold them in Vladikavkaz, in North Ossetia. It was a great life; we made quite good money, and we could rest in the autumn and then hibernate like bears in the winter. But since the 1990s, all that has changed. There's no regular work, and my husband doesn't do anything interesting anymore. Don't even ask about me. As for our children, they're growing up with no education, like idiots."

Lisa would like to continue telling me about their hard life, but one or another of the brothers constantly interrupts us, and then Said comes back from his tour of duty.

Now it's his turn to talk. He speaks with rasping breaths, as if each word were his last. "We have no real role in this conflict. The *gantemirovtsy,* as I see it, are simply middle-class men who've had enough of the war and don't want to fight or steal. They simply want to leave home in the morning and come back quietly at night, like any normal person with a job. The problem is that we're being used for something completely different. We've been thrown in between the Russians, the *boyviki,* and the Wahhabis, so that we'll all rise up one against the other," he exclaims with disgust. "As for their so-called leader, Gantemirov, he'll never be an influential figure. The Russians let him out of prison, and they'll put him right back in just as soon as he appears to be distancing himself from their position."

In mid-December 1999, Said-Mogamed signed a six-month contract, which gave him the right, as a militiaman, to carry a weapon. His role would be to maintain order, in cooperation with the Federal forces, and punish any criminal act committed in the "liberated territories." From the Russians, he received a fur-lined winter uniform, a riot stick, and a Kalachnikov. As for salary, he has received none. It was mentioned in his contract, but the amount was not specified.

What does a "Gantemirov man" spend his day doing? According to Said-Mogamed, very little. "Mornings, we assemble between nine o'clock and ten-thirty in the municipal police headquarters, depending on when the chief of police gets up. Then we spend the day walking about in the streets with no precise duties. Checking identity papers? What's the use of that? Why would I ask to see a driver's papers, even if I suspected something, when I know full well that you can buy absolutely anything in the market, from simple diplomas to drivers' licenses to every kind of weapon. No, the *gantemirovtsy* have only one thing to do: Stand at the intersections and smile."

The former watermelon farmer is disappointed with his volunteer militia, but he also has harsh words for his colleagues: "All my colleagues are drunk from morning to night. They really have nothing better to do. And they think about one thing only—stealing as much as they possibly can. When they witness Chechens or Russians violating the law, they do nothing at all. They close their eyes. The other day, I arrested someone who was using a state-owned bus for private business. I took him to the *kommandantura*. The next morning, he disappeared into thin air. My Russian colleagues let him get away, for money, of course! No, what we need is a period of the iron hand, for five years at least."

The *gantemirovtsy* are the most glaring example of the Chechens' uneasy situation. On the one hand, the Russians accuse them of "having *boyviki* sympathies" which, according to Said-

Magomed, is true for half the force. On the other, the *boyviki* don't seem to understand the *gantemirovtsy*. "They can't accept that we can be Chechen and want order to reign, but without the war," Said-Magomed explains dryly. And yet, none of the Chechen militiamen would knowingly fire on the *boyviki*. "What the Russians show on television, with the men from our forces on the front line in Grozny, that's a pure myth," he mutters. "When they ask us to go and fight in the capital, no one volunteers. We have on occasion fired from far away in the direction of the *boyviki* positions, but that's all. Not one of us would dare take up arms against them, mainly out of a fear of reprisals. We all know each other. On the Russian side, nobody wants to be sent into that nightmare of a capital, either. I even saw a man from the SOBR* shoot himself in the foot so that he wouldn't have to go."

Said-Magomed insists that every household has weapons. The idea of having to "turn in your arms" he finds amusing, even surrealistic. "Who would willingly turn in a gun when it represents something of value? Nobody at all, not in these times."

Said-Magomed can't really say why he wanted anything to do with this "dirty work." "No doubt because there wasn't any other," his wife interjects, in a low voice. This is the only question that he has trouble answering. He makes a graceful escape from the dilemma by replying with a genuine smile, "I don't know. I love music, beauty, and dance. In my heart, I'm neither a *boyvik* nor a Gantemirov man. I'm a man of order, and my dream is that my

---

* Elite troops of the Russian Ministry of the Interior.

daughter will become a ballerina.... I'd like to see as many flowers in Grozny as there used to be on the first of May. As things are now, we'll be lucky if it's a first of April," he concludes, sipping his tea.

⌒

We arrived in Starye Atagi by car, and we're back again at Laulli's, where we spent several days two months ago, at the beginning of December. The daughters bring me up-to-date on all the latest developments. They make me feel as though I am a member of the family. Teresa, the eldest, gave birth at last to twins; the two tiny forms are wrapped in blankets and rest delicately on the square pillow of the big bed. They are so small that I don't notice them right away when I enter the room. Two more mouths to feed! And yesterday, the gas was turned on. Now the family is less dependent on the wood stove in the living room and can cook in the real kitchen. That's it for the good news.

I know the rest, the inevitable wartime disasters. A neighbor appears, wrapped up in a long gray mohair scarf; she tells me how her twenty-eight-year-old son, married and the father of three children, was killed in a hail of artillery fire at the end of December. Laulli and his neighbors wonder why the Chechen refugees in Ingushetia don't come together and organize to make their voices heard. They also say that Gantemirov came in person to Starye Atagi to try to push through the creation of a new para Federal militia. He met with no success. "Here, no one likes him," Laulli snorts.

"In Grozny, our trenches are so close to each other that we can talk across them. In Russian, of course. We hear the Russians laugh, drink, and even watch television in the shelter of their BTRs. Sometimes, when one of their planes is flying over and we're trying to bring it down, they get all excited and give us advice: 'Thirty meters to the left, fifteen to the right!' I heard that once they even started shooting at their own plane because they were afraid a bomb would drop on their heads! Anything is possible when the positions are only twenty meters apart," Edik tells me. He has just returned to Starye Atagi, and he's still in a state of shock from his wounds.

Five weeks after his arrival in Grozny, the young and inexperienced fighter broke both his legs while jumping from a roof. He had been posted there as a sniper and was fleeing a bombardment. As a result, he has not been able to avenge the death of his younger brother, who was killed in November by a Russian bomb as he was walking in the forest, searching for wood.

"I'm twenty-nine, and my brother was twenty-seven. After his death, I couldn't look my sister-in-law or my nieces and nephews in the face. I had to take vengeance for him. So I decided to join a group of combatants charged with the defense of the city. When this dirty war began, I never intended to fight. I'm a shepherd myself. But, today, I'm waiting for one thing only—to get these two casts off and get back as soon as I can to Grozny." He is speaking in a low voice in poor Russian, before a crowd of his six brothers, two sisters, and their children and neighbors, who are pouring in as the news of his return spreads.

It's warm in the one-room house, which is still without electricity. Edik's face is emaciated, his eyes have black circles under them, and his pupils make him appear feverish. He is seated on a sofa with his two legs, in their plaster casts, resting on a chair in front of him. From the adjoining room comes the sound of masculine voices chanting a prayer in thanks for his return.

"In Grozny, there's really nothing left to eat. Occasionally, someone will bring in canned food from outside, but that's really all," he says. "But one thing is certain: Not one single Russian soldier has gotten inside the city, Not one! However, I did see a group of young Russian recruits—fifteen or so—who simply surrendered so that they wouldn't have to fight anymore. The guys were starving, and they told us that they were given one can of rations a day for two, but that they could only manage to eat it if the volunteer troops didn't steal it first."

The listeners are drinking in his words.

Two houses away, Zarima tells me how she also managed to get out of the capital. Two days ago, she left on foot with a group of women. They took the only corridor that was still open, the control post of Staraya Sunzha, northeast of Grozny: "They only let women in and out, and they search all their bags. The only men they let in must have proof, stamped in their passport, that they live in Grozny. I didn't see a single one leave," she explains.

Zarima has just spent a week of pure hell searching for her wounded brother in the cellars of the capital. She was unable to find him. "No one can stay on the streets for more than a minute because of the continual shelling," she says. "The only ones who go outside are the *boyviki*. Everyone else stays hunkered down in the cellars with no information at all from the outside world."

A few kilometers away, in Chiri Yurt, Arbi has also just come back home from the capital. He, however, intends to go back to Grozny with food and medical supplies for the fighting forces. A former policeman, Arbi is second-in-command of the Eastern Front, in charge of procurement. He has worked out a clever arrangement with the local miller: The miller gives Arbi sacks of flour that he exchanges elsewhere for sugar and other staples. The two men have agreed to settle up when the war is over.

Arbi tells me about one incident in mid-January 2000 when he passed through the control post of Staraya Sunzha with a car full to bursting with food. "I had to pay the soldiers off. They demanded 2,600 rubles [a little bit more than $100] and pretended they thought that the food was all going to the civilian population!"

On January 21, Arbi witnessed an important battle between Federals and Chechens. Two hundred Russians are thought to have perished that day, and even now their bodies are still lying about, pecked at by birds and torn apart by dogs.

"Our troops would very much like to salvage the weapons of the dead. And the Russians are supposed to go out and collect the bodies of their fallen comrades, but, in fact, no one on either side is moving. They fear for their own lives. On the day I left the city, the *boyviki* were going to try using lassos to get hold of the dead Russians' weapons."

⌒

I have just spent a terrible night at Starye Atagi. The sounds of the bombardment shattered the night, tearing me from my sleep. The windows vibrated incessantly. At each salvo, I huddled more tightly under the covers, as if my body were absorbing imaginary blows.

This morning, we are crossing back over the suspension bridge spanning the Argun River on our way to Novye Atagi to see if we can find Mumadi Saidayev, chief of the Chechen general staff and the right-hand man of Aslan Maskhadov. In the cars, everybody is listening to the tortured songs of the imam Elin Sultanov, a Chechen who was assassinated in Odessa in 1996. Sultanov sang in Russian, so that he would be understood by both peoples. He sang of the honor of the Chechen warrior, of the imam Shamil,* of independence, of the magnificent landscape of the Caucasus, and of blood shed by young Russians and Chechens. He accompanies his husky voice with the infectious rhythms of his guitar. Islam knows all his melodies by heart.

According to the Chechen high command, the Russian positions have hardly moved at all for a month. "They're still at Staro-promyslovskii [in the suburbs of Grozny], as they were in December," Mumadi Saidayev confirms. He is spending several

---

* In the middle of the nineteenth century, imam Shamil defied the Russians, using Islam to spur the mountain people of Dagestan and Chechnya to rise against the Russian forces. His goal was the creation of an Islamic state.

hours in a private house in Novye Atagi. Without enthusiasm, he gives his own version of recent political developments in Moscow, namely, the surprise resignation, on December 31, of President Boris Yeltsin. "Putin wants to become president, and he will certainly succeed. No doubt about that," he says. "But he won't be able to end the war, because that would imply that it has been fought for nothing. Furthermore, if he stopped the war now, he wouldn't win the election. The rapid successes that the generals promised him haven't materialized. But Putin is searching about for a way out of this conflict. He'd like to get out with his head held high."

The traffic in dead bodies seems to worry Saidayev more, however. "We don't speculate with the bodies the way they do. When they kill a Chechen, they never turn over the cadaver without being paid. And then Russians also mine corpses so that they will explode in the presence of their families. It's a way of killing even more Chechens."

He spreads out an immense map of Chechnya on the frozen earth. It was stolen from a Russian officer, and it shows the number and names of the Russian units marked in red, green, and blue. "This war is a cross between a war of position and a guerilla war. It's not in our interest to remain stationary, facing the Russians for long periods, as we do in Grozny. We should use surprise attacks in small groups. We must constantly change our tactics," says Mumadi, thinking out loud. "When they move around, the Russians try never to carry many munitions with them, so that in case of an ambush, we won't be able to get hold of their supplies."

Sometimes the rebel chief of staff visits the combatants; several days ago, he was in Grozny. "Over there, I always hear the same refrain: 'We'd rather die than let the Russians take Grozny!' I always give them the same answer: 'Children, our goal is not that you should die in the city, but that you should kill as many Russians as possible. So stop anticipating your own deaths!'"

The sky is clear, not a cloud on the horizon. It snowed during the night, and this morning the children of Chiri Yurt are having the time of their lives. Near the central market, they're bombarding each other with snowballs.

A Russian army barricade stands some two hundred meters away—two blocks of concrete and two tanks, their guns pointed menacingly in the direction of the village. They mark the boundary between the "liberated" territories of the north and the "rebel" foothills of the southern mountains.

The stream of refugees has not flowed only from Chechnya to Ingushetia since the beginning of Operation Antiterrorist; a real migratory movement has developed within the interior of Chechnya. First, while the Federals were refraining from bombing the mountain regions, the refugees moved south; then when the mid-December bombings began, they migrated north. Now the inhabitants of towns and villages such as Shatoy and Itum Kali are trying to find shelter in the "liberated territories" of the wide plains leading up to Grozny; but for the last seven days, no one has been allowed to pass through the control post separating Chiri Yurt (liberated zone) from Duba Yurt (combat zone), where Vakha

Arsanov, vice president of the rebel republic, is said to be entrenched. For some unknown reason, the Federal troops refused to open a corridor that would have allowed the thousands of refugees massed at Duba Yurt to cross over into the relative safety of the liberated zone. All week these helpless souls have been under the constant fire of artillery and combat aircraft. At last, this morning, the two BTRs slowly moved aside. In one day, more than 2,000 refugees have crossed the border in the direction of Chiri Yurt.

Leyla is sitting beside her husband in his tractor. Her hair is disheveled under a red wool scarf, her lips chapped by the biting cold. She holds her two youngest children in her arms. She has no more strength. "I can barely bring myself to tell what we have just lived through. Twelve days without a break in our cellar in Shatoy. We had nothing left to eat. At last, we got to Duba Yurt, thinking that we'd find some way to go north, but we got stuck here, trapped," she stutters, beside herself with emotion.

A little further on, Issa is having a hard time changing gears in his old Soviet Zhigouli. The car is filled to the brim with as many possessions as he could rescue when he fled the bombardments. His fate is even more tragic then Leyla's. Less than a week ago, he lost his wife and four children in an air attack on the village of Dachu Borzoy. Issa escaped only because he happened not to be at home when the powerful bomb exploded, killing everyone. From the wreckage, he could retrieve only the body of his twenty-six-year-old wife, Marietta. He gathered all his courage and placed her in the car, on the top of rugs, chairs, a table, and the television set, and set off for the north. The family had just fled south in mid-

November because they thought the conflict would never spread to the mountains. Issa wanted to return to bury his wife in the cemetery of her home town, but for five days he was unable to pass through the control post at Duba Yurt and he was forced to bury her there. "In the end I did what all the others do," he says quietly. "I took a shovel and dug her grave in a vegetable garden in Duba Yurt. There was nothing else to do. I couldn't wait any longer." According to Issa, dozens of others in the same situation have had to bury their family members in Duba Yurt, simply because the checkpoint was closed.

Wild rumors are circulating within the traumatized population about the mistreatment of Chechen civilians by Russian troops at these highway control points. Injured Chechens often disappear without a trace, or they're accused of being combatants and die mysteriously "as a result of their wounds." This information has been confirmed by Issa Madayev, the former administrative head of Chiri Yurt and co-president of the Committee for the Liberation of Persons Detained in the First War: "More than a thousand persons, who were arrested while passing through checkpoints, are now in cellars in the hands of the Russians. And these are only the civilians. We are trying to get them back."

Keeping track of these "disappearances" and compiling lists of names is also the responsibility of Khamzat Bibulatov, the general military prosecutor of the Republic of Chechnya, and of his assistant. The two men are temporarily occupying an apartment in Chiri Yurt. They have a few furnishings, including an antique typewriter.

"We are watching out for human rights violations, and there

have been a certain number. Even in wartime, the laws of the *charia* and the constitution must be respected. That means that all those who collaborate with the occupier will be punished," Khamzat states solemnly. He is a former vice minister of the MVD (Ministry of the Interior) under Maskhadov, president of the military tribunal under Yandarbiev, and a simple combatant under Dudayev. "We also prosecute marauders and thieves. However, as we have nowhere to imprison them, we use them to dig trenches."

≙

I am waiting for Islam. He has set off in the direction of Urus-Martan to get papers that will allow him to pass through the control posts without problems. It has become more and more difficult to move about, especially for men; they may disappear at any moment, spirited off by the increasingly suspicious Federals. Our traveling together, therefore, has become dangerous for me—and also for him. I try to explain to him that he shouldn't take useless risks simply to keep me company. Because I plan to go to Grozny—and we are receiving less and less information about the city—it would be better if he stayed put somewhere and waited for me. He answers stubbornly that he "came [into Chechnya] with me and that he will go out the same way." But, at last, he agrees that I can travel without him if I find a woman or an old man* who agrees to escort me.

---

* At that time, only men of sixty and above could still move about freely and without raising suspicions.

Islam is always a little melodramatic; as he left the house, he warned that "if I'm not back before noon tomorrow, you can consider me dead." I know that he doesn't really expect to die. This is his way of assuring me that he will come back no matter what and that I shouldn't worry myself sick about him.

I am worried nevertheless, because eleven o'clock has passed and he still isn't back; moreover, I am planning to leave the next day, having found companions for my trip. I have even written Islam a note in which I explain with whom and for how long I am traveling to Grozny. Elena will keep the note in her bosom.

In the afternoon, Anzor tells me amazing stories about the *bizness* of the Russian soldiers who were held hostage from 1996 to 1999, after the end of the first war. The conversation is constantly interrupted by the noisy arrivals and departures of people coming to Anzor for advice. He offers them lengthy counsel in Chechen. Despite the ragged quality of his account, I understand that when Vladimir Rushaylo—then only a vice minister—wanted to become Minister of the Interior, he had to create favorable publicity by persuading the Chechens to release hostages. One of Anzor's friends was "deep in this business"; he proposed that Anzor buy the Russian soldiers for $8,000 apiece "just to keep them a little" before sending them to Nalchik, where they would be freed; the business would bear the stamp of the "Special Operation of the Ministry of the Interior." Anzor would be paid in advance; the necessary money, which would come from the highest levels of the Russian state, would be passed to Anzor by circuitous means. Anzor even alludes to Boris Berezovski, an influential millionaire in Yeltsin's Kremlin, who has often been accused of dabbling in illegal operations.

Anzor lets out a big laugh, which makes his glasses jump on his nose; he folds them and places them on his typewriter.

"The day before yesterday," he says, "two people from the village came to tell me that they were holding two Russian soldiers hostage and that they wanted my help in *selling* them. Of course, I refused outright, and I urged them to free the two Russians immediately. But if you only knew how many young Russian deserters rush here, to my house. They'll do anything to avoid returning to the army. It breaks my heart, but I am obliged to return them to the authorities."

⌒

This morning, I left early for Grozny with Vakha, a pensioner, and Larissa, an "ex-combatant," as she describes herself. We plan to pass through the control post at Staraya Sunzha, the only crossing point we have been able to find. Islam has returned, but without the papers he wanted; we have agreed that he will wait for me somewhere in the region. We formulate a strategy in case I do not return on the appointed day, but we give ourselves a margin of five days. Islam had wanted to make his own way to Grozny and meet me there, but I talked him out of it; Grozny is not the sort of city in which to rendezvous. Who knows what state it will be in? We set off, by way of Shaly and Argun, and change cars four times along the way.

For hours now, in subzero temperatures, about a dozen women have been trying to persuade the soldiers of the MVD, who are in charge of the first control post in Staraya Sunzha, near Grozny, to allow them in. The military activity on all sides is intense. The suburb of Microrayon, through which the Russian forces are currently attempting to penetrate the capital from the north, lies less than a kilometer away. The noise of artillery shelling, together with the sound of helicopters and planes, never stops. It's a kind of permanent fireworks to which no one pays attention.

"As of yesterday, no one gets through except for women with children and men more than sixty years old who are registered residents of Staraya Sunzha," a big open-faced fellow explains, as he adjusts his mittens. He is wearing the uniform of the Russian militia and has a rifle slung across his chest. His colleague—small and stocky with three days' growth of beard and blue eyes that peer out from under a black wool cap—exhibits less patience. The gaggle of women pester him with questions in Russian, then comment among themselves in Chechen, a language he doesn't understand. It's a dialogue of the deaf.

"So when will this war be over?" asks one of the women.

"Don't ask me that. Ask one of your own men," one of the guards shoots back in an annoyed tone. "Because it's your husbands, your brothers, your sons, and your nephews who are fighting over there," he adds as he indicates with a large gesture the direction of the explosions.

"No, they're not! Our husbands—as you call them—are refugees just like us, victims of this war."

"It's the Wahhabis who are fighting, not our men," another woman argues.

"Then go back to where you came from. Try to find your husbands. You've no reason to be here, in a combat zone. Go on, we're not going to let you through," the grouchy Russian insists. "What's more, you have no valid reason for wanting to go to Grozny. It's too dangerous."

The women can put forward any conceivable argument—say she's returning to check on her family, or that she'll be back in less than an hour, or that she's going to a funeral or, even that she left her sick and aged mother alone in Grozny a month ago. The Russian guards will not budge.

An old woman is squatting in the snow, drawing strange geometrical figures on the ground with her frozen fingers. From time to time, she stifles little sobs with her black wool scarf. She has lost her identity papers and now she cannot get back to her home in Staraya Sunzha. For the moment she has to endure the humiliating wait.

More military vehicles are on the roads: Camouflaged trucks, some empty, some filled with haggard young men, BMPs and MTRs.* The traffic in the direction of Grozny never stops. The drivers have all stuffed bulletproof vests against their left front windows. "Protection from lateral fire," Vakha explains. On two occasions, soldiers in *maskhalat* garb—large, snow-white overalls

---

* Tanks with treads or wheels, respectively.

worn as camouflage over their combat uniforms—pass by slowly. The white veils that cover their faces make them look like desert Bedouins. In another truck, twenty or so *nayomniki,** who appear to be returning from their positions, are awaiting orders. They're having a smoke, and the two recruits in charge of the control post watch them enviously. At least half the volunteers have Asian features: High cheekbones and slanting eyes; they all wear brand new grenade launchers on their backs. As they get out of the truck, one of them slips and falls flat on the ice. Stifled laughter breaks out among the crowd of women on the other side of the barrier.

A thin scarfless woman carrying two heavy sacks, her face swollen with tears and bruises, threads her way towards me through the throng. She has just spent two weeks in Grozny searching for her husband, and she has escaped from the capital with great difficulty. "Having survived I don't know how many bombardments, we finally arrived, risking our lives, at the post at Staraya Sunzha," she explains with difficulty. "But I never could have imagined how hard it would be to get out of that particular hell. For several days now, they've had a woman from the MVD who searches you from head to foot and takes pleasure in humiliating you. She looked into my tights and my socks and kept repeating over and over that I had the eyes of a sniper, that I must surely have been fighting."

Zulikhane's beautiful eyes blaze with hatred. The friend who was accompanying her has been dispatched to an unknown locale

---

* Volunteers, in Russian.

because her passport was apparently no longer valid. "This functionary from the MVD discovered a photo of my friend's husband, and she made her tear it up right then and there. She said he looked like a bandit!" Looking more closely at Zulikhane, I suddenly realize that she is pregnant.

All the money that Zulikhane had in the world, some 50 rubles [$1.50] was in the pocket of her friend's anorak. Now she has nothing and she has no idea how she will get back to her home near Urus-Martan. I give her 100 rubles, and she is overcome with gratitude. When she realizes that I am a foreigner, she asks me why I want to get to Grozny. I explain that I am a journalist. She has an idea, which she proposes to me and my companions. Two weeks earlier, when she was searching for a way into the surrounded capital, she passed through the hamlet of Alkhan Kala, where she knows a smuggler. She offers to take us there this evening.

⌒

We have to hurry to cover as much ground as possible before the six o'clock curfew. We change cars at least six times before we arrive back at Starye Atagi. I have the impression I'm going in circles, but I'm excited and eager to arrive at our destination. I would like to stop and see Islam, to tell him that things didn't work out at Staraya Sunzha and that we have had to change our plans, but there isn't time.

Beside the highway, at the edge of Starye Atagi, the four of us attempt to hitchhike. There isn't much chance of getting a ride. Cars are few, and most of them are full. We decide to separate: I will stay with Larissa, and Zulikhane will go on with Vakha. At last, a car stops and we jump in. Vakha, who lives in Starye Atagi, has proposed that we meet in the central square of the next village, Goyty.

The passengers in our car are simple farmers. I am in the back, squeezed up against an old woman; her two sons are in the front seat. They are driving very slowly, and one of them keeps turning around to stare at Larissa. He's like an inquisitor. I say nothing, but I sense that he is asking her all kinds of questions about us, where we're going, what we're up to. The odor of sweat coming from the woman next to me makes me feel ill.

When we finally arrive in Goyty, night has already fallen. Here and there, the market stalls are illuminated with gasoline lamps. I am worried about Vakha and Zulikhane; I have a premonition that they weren't able to get a ride. Larissa is more optimistic. She stays on the sidewalk and watches the cars go by, while I take refuge in a grocery store to try to unthaw my feet; no matter how hard I knock them together, they have no feeling at all. Many young Russian soldiers enter the shop, always accompanied by a Chechen. They buy beer, various liquors, chocolate, and candy, as if they had something to celebrate. Some of them shoot me a look out of the corner of their eyes. I am worried that they will speak to me; I try to look aloof, and keep my gaze fixed on the blackness outside, where I can just barely make out the stocky shape of Larissa in her long leather coat.

Vakha and Zulikhane still haven't turned up. The curfew must have prevented them from leaving. They've probably gone back to Vakha's house for the night, I tell myself to quiet my anxiety. I am exasperated by the thought of having lost them. Vakha was the pillar of our little foursome. I need his counsel and his patience. Now I'm alone with Larissa, whom I barely know. She's only twenty-six, but she appears older; she's a "combatant," as she admits with barely disguised pride. She's large and heavy, with the hands of a workman. Her dark hair, held back at the base of her neck with a barrette, escapes constantly from her purple headscarf. It contrasts with her bright blue eyes and her white teeth, which have no visible gold fillings.

We must find somewhere to sleep and quickly. I go out to discuss the situation with my companion, but she has already found a bed from someone whom she met in the street. It occurs to me that Islam would never handle matters this way.

The man lives next to the market. We head down a dark little alley and arrive at a large house, apparently divided among several families. I check that Larissa hasn't explained to our host who we are or why we're here. One can't be too careful.

But as soon as we enter the house, I feel comforted by the stranger's humble Chechen family. Once again, our hosts will sleep on the floor and give us their bed. After we've wolfed down a delicious macaroni soup, the older brother, cigarette dangling from his lips, tells me how, after ten quiet years in Stavropol, he was chased from his home by the local authorities. "They said to us, 'Well, now that you [the Chechens] have your own territory, with your own independent leader [Dzhokhar Dudayev], go back to where you came from. There's no more use for you here!'" At that point, dozens of families left for Chechnya; but for many of them, it was an unfamiliar land. They had not set foot there since their exile to Kazakhstan.

"At that time," the man continues, "it was easy to buy property in Grozny. Houses were relatively cheap because most of the Russians were leaving the city. But already there was no work, everything was going to the dogs. We could see the collapse that was coming."

During the two wars, this father of six brought his family to live at his parents' house in Goyty, where we are spending the night. Like many Chechens who have been forced out of their homes, he is waiting patiently for the end of the war or for a chance to return to Grozny to check the state of his property; only then will he decide whether to stay or to leave for good. "Even though we're tired of these comings and goings, we'll head for Russia," he says softly.

⌒

The next morning, after a sound night's sleep under a comforter as heavy as a stone, and a breakfast of hot tea, homemade rolls, and some leftover spicy noodles, Larissa and I leave to find a ride to Urus-Martan. We vaguely remember what Zulikhane had told us about the smuggler in Alkhan Kala. We'll try to go there and find him ourselves; but first, we're going to stop in Alkhan Yurt, where Larissa has family who may be able to help us.

After changing cars twice, we arrive at the outskirts of Alkhan Yurt. At the huge roundabout, the young MVD men on duty watch us closely, half smiles on their faces. Once again, I hope desperately not to draw their attention; but Larissa strides forward with her head held high, her blue eyes fixed straight ahead.

Larissa is tough. In mid-January, she was still in Grozny and left only because "the boys [the *boyviki*] made me." She lets out a hard laugh. The *boyviki* wanted her to return to Novye Atagi to take care of her two-year-old daughter, whose father had died in Grozny two months before.

"They kept telling me, 'Go on, Larissa, get out of here. Leave us; do it for your daughter!' To which I replied, 'But what will I do, twiddling my thumbs in the village, just thinking about you?' 'You've got to go on living and have other children, Larissa. You've got to perpetuate the race,' they insisted."

So she went back to Novye Atagi and waited for a new mission. To give her something to do, the *boyviki* asked her to serve as a liaison officer in charge of counterespionage. "It wasn't bad," she concedes, "but rather boring. When I was in the city, I did a little bit of everything. I was a sniper, a cook, a nurse, an intelligence agent. It was more varied, and then there were people around."

As we arrive in Alkhan Yurt, we quicken our pace and stride along side by side down the steep road. It's so warm that Larissa takes her coat off, and I see that she's wearing a shiny wool sweater and a long sleeveless vest. Larissa has not been to the village for two years and she is determined to find out whether Malika, a distant cousin, is still living here. She asks three passers-by for "the house of Malika, the schoolteacher." They point the way without a word. In this village, which was under Russian bombardment only a week before, the locals say little.

We come to a street that looks much like the others, but has suffered somewhat more bomb damage. Larissa lets go of my arm and begins to run. I see her stop, turn to the right, and raise her hands to her face. She throws herself down in the snow and remains in a kneeling position for several seconds before crumpling to the ground.

All that remains of Malika's house is its wooden fence. Everything else is just a heap of stones already partially hidden by the most recent snowfall. To the right and to the left of the house, there's only rubble. I come up to Larissa, put my hand on her broad back and help her to her feet, murmuring, "Come on, let's go. Don't cry anymore, it's no use. Come away."

It's a shock to see Larissa cry. She has no handkerchief, and neither do I. We start back the way we came. Larissa seems to recover some of her strength and jams her fists in the pockets of her coat.

"What's the matter, my child? What's happened?" A woman is running towards us through the snow. She's in her housecoat. Larissa throws herself in the woman's arms and begins to cry. The old lady invites us in to warm up and have some tea.

We enter the ruins of a house. We had passed in front of it minutes before, but it's so dilapidated that we had failed to notice that it was inhabited. Only one room has been saved. "That's where we live," the woman explains. The "we" in question is the woman, her daughter, her daughter's husband, and their two little boys, who are sitting, good as gold, next to the stove. They're dangling their little legs from the wooden slats that serve as their bed. No one seems surprised by our intrusion. The man puts his hat on straight away and slips out for a walk. Already the water is boiling. We're given hot tea in large light green bowls. The day before, near Staraya Sunzha, I bought some little cakes that look like madeleines; I pull them out of my bag now and put them on the table. The two boys can't take their eyes off them; their silence speaks volumes. I gesture to them to help themselves. After a questioning look at their mother, each boy lifts one cake delicately to his mouth. Though they're clearly famished, they take small bites, savoring each morsel.

The two women tell us in detail about the horrors of the bombings, the Russians' entry into the village, and the harsh demands the soldiers imposed. "We didn't see anything. We hid for four days under a pile of manure. My son-in-law had taken care of everything—food reserves and air tunnels. No one noticed us. That's how we were able to escape. But almost all our neighbors disappeared. When we came out, there were bodies everywhere. We had to bury them." The old woman turns to Larissa. "As for you, Larissa, don't cry. Your Malika left the country for Russia in early November. Her house didn't collapse on her."

When she hears these happy words, Larissa's color returns and she soon recovers her fighter's voice. She smiles at me and tosses off a brave "Shall we go?" It's as if we were leaving for the beach.

As we cross the roundabout again, Larissa puts her haughty manner back on. The same soldiers are giving us the same careful looks. We quickly find a car to take us to Alkhan Kala. I had almost forgotten about Vakha and Zulikhane. Now I pray that we will find each other and continue on as a foursome.

At the top of a steep rise we come upon the large market of Alkhan Kala. On this sunny day, at least three hundred merchants

—mostly women—are standing or sitting on cardboard boxes, waiting for customers. Their merchandise is almost always the same: chewing gum, hard candy, sunflower seeds sold by the glass, butter, margarine, rice, cheap pasta, and, on occasion, sacks of sugar or flour. They also have an astonishing variety of chocolate bars—Snickers, Mars, Bounty, M&Ms.

Here, Russian soldiers are the only customers who have money and buy merchandise. They are awaited like the Messiah as they pass through town to and from their battle stations. I wander among the stalls, whose goods I already know by heart, while Larissa enters into discussion with a group of men who are busy ingesting large quantities of sunflower seeds. I know that she is trying to extract information on where the Russians are posted, how we might be able to get through to Grozny, find a smuggler, etc. From time to time, she shoots me a look out of her blue eyes, and I note that she is entirely at ease, basking in the belief that her mission is of the highest possible importance.

In this way, we learn that one of our options is to hitch a ride with the Russians. A group is bound for a place known as "Pervyi Molsovkhoz," a supremely Soviet-style abbreviation for "First Milk-Producing State Farm." Quite a large crowd of hitchhikers is already waiting for a ride. "They surely won't take everybody, even for money," I say. Larissa, ever the optimist, is sure they will.

Having made the tour of the market five or six times already, it's my turn to snack on sunflower seeds. The saleswoman pours a full glass of seeds into my pocket, and I nibble on them, spitting out the husks. As I nibble away, I notice a wagon by the side of the road. White smoke is rising from its small chimney. "A café,"

Larissa explains. We go in and order *manty*. The dumplings are swimming in an unappetizing sauce, but they're warm and therefore comforting. The young woman who appears to be the owner of the café is pleasant and speaks Russian without a trace of an accent. When we've eaten, I ask her if I can stay a bit longer in the warmth "to write." The woman, Assia, is delighted. She understands that I need a little privacy and invites me to take a place at the table in the kitchen. Larissa goes out to stand guard.

With her scarf cleverly rolled into a thin headband, her long straight skirt and matching low-cut velour top, Assia is one of the most modern young women I've met. I guess that she's in her thirties. A doctor by profession, the oldest of ten children, she worked for a while at the hospital in Rostov-on-the-Don. In 1994, her parents decided to return to their homeland in Chechnya. Assia was planning to set up a pharmacy kiosk in front of the Hospital Number 2, but her house in Grozny was twice reduced to rubble; she escaped to this suburb of the capital. "I am delighted, because tomorrow my brothers are going to install a gas stove. I'll be able to make cakes. I'm sure you'll like them!" she announces, as if I were a regular customer.

Assia has no regular customers. Most locals are too poor to eat out, even here. Despite her bright smile, I can tell Assia's life is hard. The "café" is tiny. Assia washes her dishes by rinsing them in small basins. She passes a moth-eaten sponge over the oilcloth in her kitchen. From time to time, I glimpse her niece, Maaka, through the half-open door. The girl is busy greeting patrons, sorting the trash, cutting bread. She looks like a little elf.

The caravan has been stationed on the central square for three years, but it was only this winter that Assia decided to transform it into a snack bar. She's a real entrepreneur. "Everyone who knows me is astonished. I've always been a pharmacist, and now here I am at the stove. But it's really quite reasonable. I've got to feed my family. I'm not at all ashamed," she explains, laughing.

She talks frankly about the relations between the local population and the Russian troops stationed on the outskirts. "The soldiers no longer want to sell us what they used to—gasoline, weapons, canned food. No, now they don't want money. What they want is drugs!"

As for the soldiers who "do the taxiing" to Molsovkhoz, she advises me strongly against them. "The Russians do business not only with the dead but also with the living. They tell us that they're not getting paid, and that they have to survive. They pretend they're running a taxi service, and then they kidnap their passengers and demand ransoms. Families can pay either in cash or in kind—a cow, a sheep, whatever is edible."

As Assia chatters away, my glance falls upon the only window, adapted to accommodate the exhaust pipe of the stove. I catch sight of Larissa running toward two people on the highway in the distance: Vakha and Zulikhane!

⌒

Saittami, the "smuggler," is making us wait. We'll spend the night at his mother's house, get up early, and start out on foot. For once, the dusk is quiet. As I fall asleep on the floor of the only heated room, I can just hear Larissa's murmured confidences. She'll plot with Saittami long into the night.

At dawn, Zulikhane leaves us, satisfied with having accomplished her mission. She is on her way home to her family in Urus-Martan. Vakha, for his part, plans to return to Starye Atagi today, where he will wait for us. Larissa is trembling with emotion at the idea of rejoining her *boyviki* "brothers." She has a thousand things to do as soon as we get to the city. Saittami laces his boots slowly. It's about six miles to Grozny.

⌒

It was barely 7:00 A.M. when the first rusted minibuses swept into the ice-covered courtyard of the Alkhan Kala hospital. The news made the rounds quickly from house to house. "The Grozny wounded have arrived!" a young boy cried at the top of his voice as he galloped through the village. We had already left.

We're in the middle of a field, on the outskirts of Alkhan Kala, when a group of children give us our first hint of that morning's event: "They've come, the *boyviki* from Grozny!" they tell us, giggling and elbowing each other in the ribs. Saittami asks them to explain just what they're jabbering about. They describe what they have witnessed in the town center. Immediately, we decide to turn back. "After all," I think to myself, "no one is waiting for me in Grozny."

When we arrive back in town, groups of bearded men with vacant eyes, their chests bristling with ammunition, are extracting themselves from the vehicles. Some of the men are wearing rugs cut up into ponchos to protect them from the cold. Most of them have draped white sheets over their battle dress for camouflage. They've even wrapped their guns in white cloth to make them blend in with the snow. The two floors of the village hospital are quickly filled with the *boyviki,* who are arriving in ever increasing numbers. Only one surgeon is on duty, a specialist in cosmetic surgery. He gets to work at once.

Outside, where it's minus thirteen degrees, the atmosphere is tense. People are greeting each other quietly; women are dabbing their tears with the corners of their scarves. There is the sound of metal upon metal as the armed men embrace. The *boyviki* who are not wounded stay outdoors, munching on bread rolls that the village residents have eagerly brought them. The crowd is growing by the minute. "Who wants a little fresh water? Roasted chicken?" an old woman asks no one in particular. She is walking around with a pail in one hand and a plastic bag full of food in the other.

At first I don't know what to make of the scene. What's going on here? Why are all the rebels here? And what are the Russians doing? I know that the Russians have us surrounded from the high ground on all sides. Surely they're watching our every movement through their field glasses. They can't be unaware of what's happening here in this hospital in so-called liberated territory.

Three or four men detach themselves from the hundreds of anonymous forms. They are young men from Bamut who come forward to ask me about Islam. I hardly have time to answer when one of them takes me by the arm and leads me towards someone whom I have trouble recognizing from behind. The man turns around: It's Khamzat, commander of the "immortal fortress."

We go off into a corner to talk quietly. Khamzat asks me what I'm doing here; I explain that I'm on my way to Grozny. His gray eyes stare into mine, and his thin lips, which seem to be frosted together, open slowly. "Don't go. I forbid you to go!" he says, in a soft stern voice, which I have never heard before. "We're all leaving Grozny. What's more, they set a trap for us; they mined the exit corridor. You haven't any reason to go in there now. Besides, we too, have mined everything for them. So you couldn't take a step there all by yourself."

"But I was going to see Lechi [Dudayev]," I reply. "He isn't with you, by any chance?"

Khamzat presses his lips together tightly. "They buried Lechi this morning."

I blanch and turn away for a second. This news is monumental. We are at a turning point in the war.

At dawn, 2,100 rebel fighters arrived here. Theoretically, this area is under Russian control. To leave Grozny, the rebels had to walk for miles through mine fields that encircle the capital. "Nine men were killed in the first fifty meters," Bashir, another commander, tells me. "We had to change our tactics and our direction to cut our losses. We couldn't avoid contact with the Russian troops. There were dead and wounded on both sides."

Among the "exiting" are more than two hundred women—combatants, cooks, and nurses—and about a hundred men from the Shamil Bassayev batallion. Those left in Grozny include the commander of the western front, Khamzat Gulyayev, assisted by

Akhmed Zakayev and Aslambek Ismaylov, the director of operations in the capital.

"We left Grozny to take care of our wounded and to carry on our mission elsewhere," explains Khamzat. The Bamut commander had been stationed in Grozny since last December. He led a column of 190 men. "It was all for nothing," he says with regret. "I'm ashamed, ashamed to be here in this village, ashamed to put its residents in danger. But I'm especially ashamed to have lost so many young men in an unsuccessful campaign. Now I must go to their parents. What am I going to say to them? I've had enough of these politicians and of these Wahhabis I've been fighting the last few years. Now we're condemned to fight on to the last. I told Shamil [Bassayev] not to go to Dagestan. But he never listens to anybody. Those who come along after the war will be even more aggressive. Behind us, we've left so many dead bodies, not only our own men but also civilians. There's nobody left to bury them."*

When they left Grozny, the combatants chose not to bring along their numerous prisoners of war. Instead, they exchanged their hostages, many of whom had been in captivity since the beginning of the Russian offensive on the capital, for arms. During their retreat, the Chechens managed to destroy twenty-four pieces of artillery abandoned by the Russians. They also took numerous "trophies," including arms, ammunition, and documents. But those trophies were a sad consolation for such carnage.

Khamzat tells me that Shamil Bassayev is among the wounded.

---

* In May 2000, I learned that Khamzat had died of wounds suffered during the fighting in the village of Komsomolskoye in March 2000.

Bassayev stepped on a mine this morning and is said to be undergoing an operation. I know how important this piece of information is; if I call it in to my newspaper, the story will be picked up right away by all the international agencies. But what if it isn't true? What if I make a mistake? What if it's not Bassayev but someone else? The only way to be sure is to go and see, with my own eyes, whether the man is really wounded.

The hospital is alive with intense activity. Every room holds at least four wounded, and sometimes as many as five or six. The hospital is pathetically underequipped. Apart from metal beds, there's nothing; medications are almost nonexistent. Blood is everywhere, seeping through the dressings, dripping onto the floor. Nurses are running from floor to floor in search of clean syringes. I go from room to room in an attempt to carry out a methodical search; I look into all the faces, but there are too many of them, and they all look alike! I step over some bodies, turn others over. Nurses hand me water bottles to hold up to the lips of groaning men. I agree to help. Tourniquets need to be tightened. I squeeze muscled forearms covered in bruises.

Although I've lost track of my route, I continue my search. I've already been looking for an hour and a half. There's just one place left: The operating room. In the corridor leading to it, the faces are even more grave. No one pays any attention to me or prevents me from continuing. I open the door, and I see him. Without a doubt, it's Bassayev, with his sad eyes and delicate nose. His face is ashen. He turns to look at me, and two other pairs of eyes turn my way, those of the nurse and the doctor in his green tunic, his forearms red with blood. They're getting ready to amputate Shamil

Basayev's right foot at the ankle. On the table, Basayev's half-nude body appears to be covered with metal fragments. They shimmer like the scales of a fish. I close the door.

It's now close to two o'clock, and most of the *boyviki* have already left the hospital by foot, car, or minibus; they'll stay in private houses in town until their own families can locate them. Vakha, who fortunately has not yet left for Starye Atagi, is waiting for me outdoors in the courtyard, and we have a moment to exchange a few words about the situation.

Several hundred meters away, near the central market, where we spent the day yesterday, Russian tanks and armored cars continue their incessant comings and goings. Although the village has no *kommandantura,* it has already been "cleansed" three times by the Russians. I go back to Saittami's, intending to write up an article and dictate it to Moscow via my satellite phone. My phone's batteries are dead, but Islam has invented a system to power the phone through a car battery. I don't know where we'll find a car, but we'll solve that problem when we get to it.

Saittami's mother advises me to go to the house across the street, where my things have been transferred. My hostess is now Iakha, a 26-year-old woman who lives alone with her grandmother; the old lady has been paralyzed for a decade and is rumored to be 120. Vakha rejoins me here and takes advantage of a moment of calm to nap beside the stove. Larissa has disappeared. I haven't seen her since this morning, at the hospital, where she was offering aid and comfort to her comrades.

As night is falling, I can't help returning to the hospital, which is only a hundred meters from the house. The same furious activity is going on, but now each room has fewer patients. Still no movement from the Russians. It's strange. When are they going to start firing?

"They're so afraid of us that they'll never dare to show themselves here," explains Magomed, commander of one of the sectors of Grozny. I have run into him in one of the hospital corridors. "This just goes to show that we could make an assault anywhere in Russia. And that's what we're going to do, we're not going to hold back! It's time they had a taste of their own medicine!"

Magomed's fighters agree. Tzhu, a square-shouldered young soldier in a fur-lined uniform, looks at me stonily; her face is impossible to read. "As long as there's one Chechen left on this earth, they will not take us," she says.

I can hear the incessant throbbing of helicopters and warplanes in the distance. They're still not coming after us. But bombs are falling at an accelerated rhythm in the distance, over Grozny.

"We're going to leave the city to them, and they're going to continue to bomb it well after we're gone, because they're so afraid of going in," says Magomed. "They'll plant their flag there. And then we'll counterattack. There's no other possible outcome."

At the end of the hallway, I meet another Larissa, who nonchalantly cradles a Kalachnikov. She has a small turned-up nose, clear eyes, and vermilion-colored lips, which give her a feminine appearance despite her bulky uniform. This twenty-one-year-old Chechen from Grozny is a *boyvitchka*.* "Since I was little," she says proudly, "I wanted to make the *gazovat*.† And now, here I am."

---

* Female combatant, in Russian.
† Holy war, in Chechen.

Larissa hasn't been to school in six years, since the beginning of
the present Russo-Chechen war, but she doesn't regret it. Before
hurrying off into the shadows with the others, she reflects on the
series of events that mark a war she considers "just and necessary."
"It won't stop until Allah decides it," she says calmly. "It's He who
imposes and we who dispose." As for her Russian enemies, Larissa
is without pity: "Before, we just cut their heads off. Now we have
decided to eat them." She states these words mechanically, as if
someone had stuffed the phrase into her head. It's the Wahhabis,
the Islamic radicals, who really spark her fury. "This war began,
and continues, simply because of them. If it stops against the Russians, we will continue it ourselves. It's what our ancestors predicted since the beginning of time. According to them, there's still
one war left for us to win, the war of sabers, the ultimate war
between those who believe and the others, that is, the Wahhabis."

She adds impudently, "I will stay here in the field as long as the
war continues. Even if my brothers or some other person from the
teip orders me to stay at home, I won't listen to them."

Larissa is risking her life with the *boyviki* who have left Grozny.
Neither her father nor her three brothers, all of whom live in
Katayama, a suburb of Grozny, authorized her to leave her family
and go out to make the *gazovat*. There was, therefore, only one solution to get around the interdiction—marry a fighter. In October,
when the war was just beginning, Larissa became engaged to a young
man who was traveling through Dagestan on business. She recalls
him today with the greatest scorn: "My fiancé was a Wahhabi, and I
was hypnotized by him. Like all the others from his clique, he
thought only about money. Those people have sold themselves."

In early November, she was "kidnapped" by a group of *boyviki*. One of them decided to take her for his wife, and the marriage was immediately pronounced. In Chechnya and Ingushetia, "stealing" your wife from her family is common practice. Many women take a certain pride in being "stolen," even if they were initially taken against their will. "Today, the only thing I'm afraid of is not the bombs or the Russians, but the possibility that my former fiancé will come looking for me," Larissa says.

But Larissa needn't worry. She is well protected. Her husband, who is eighteen years her senior, is a well-known fighter who was wounded slightly as he was leaving Grozny.

"I don't love him, but everybody respects him, and thanks to him, I have the right to participate in the war." Larissa doesn't seem to mind that her freedom is relative. For the moment, there is no talk of children, "or they will be little *mujahedeen* who will have only one idea in their heads: Vengeance."

Larissa won't admit to being tired out by the long nights under bombardment or by the marches across rivers and fields as the front advances and retreats. "I will continue to help the *boyviki* as best I can. In the city, I made bread and delivered arms, and sometimes my husband permitted me to shoot," she says, taking out her Soviet-made pistol. Nothing in the world would convince her to exchange her uniform for a headscarf.

⌂

Last night, sleep wouldn't come. Darkness seemed to last forever. What was in store for us on that second day in Alkhan Kala?

Would another group of *boyviki* arrive during the night, as the rebel fighters had predicted the previous day? How would the Russians react to this flood of rebels passing under their noses?

The rebels waited all night for a minibus that would take them to the mountains in the south. In the street, ghostly figures, barely visible in their camouflage, stood silently in small groups, ready for departure.

This morning, in the courtyard of the hospital, the snow is stained red with blood. Last night, another 2,000 rebel soldiers left Grozny with their wounded and their dead. Rudimentary stretchers lay abandoned on the ground. Five cadavers are lying on their backs, their faces covered with dirty sheets. Among them lies the body of Aslambek Ismaylov, the same person about whom Khamzat of Bamut said yesterday, "Happily, he is still among the living." From time to time, one of Ismaylov's soldiers lifts the corner of his shroud, contemplates the frozen features for a few seconds, and falls to his knees for a quick prayer.

Khamzat Guelayev and his men also arrived during the night; they, too, had suffered enormous losses in the retreat. "They were huge on both sides," says Zelimkhan, a red-haired fighter. "The corridor we took was a real trap. The Russians knew that we were going to leave. They had mined everything. I've stopped counting the number of my men who've lost their legs."

Most of the wounded sent to the Alkhan Kala hospital, more than a hundred of them, are suffering from injuries to their lower limbs.

"At Grozny, we got to the point where we looked at each other and asked ourselves who would be next," Zelimkhan recalls. "Of course, we were ready to die, and we still are, but our losses were too high. We lost fifteen to twenty men a day from artillery and 'aerosol bombs.'"

Zelimkhan thinks that Russia's interim president, Vladimir Putin, called for the siege because he needed a victory before the presidential election on March 26. "He had to take the city before that date. That's why we left," Zelimkhan explains. "There could even have been a secret agreement between Aslan Maskhadov and the Kremlin authorities."

As we're talking, a helicopter appears in the gray sky; Zelimkhan barely has time to finish his sentence before rockets begin to shower down on the hospital. "Disperse, all of you, disperse!" a man shouts to anyone who will listen. Women and children run for shelter. The *boyviki* fail to answer with automatic fire; they are frozen in place. An old man leaning on his cane takes the young combatants to task: "Don't you see that the Russians are observing you?" he says, pointing toward the mountains. "At least take off your uniforms before you go out!" He attacks a smaller group angrily: "The ones who arrived yesterday were more disciplined. Today, they're all Wahhabis. They don't listen to anything. We're going to have problems."

Since Monday night, the flow of rebels leaving Grozny hasn't stopped. Now the village is in the grip of fear. Around eleven o'clock, faint with hunger, I go to the market in the vague hope that I will be able to get a cup of tea. A heavy padlock secures the door of Assia's wagon. The market, which was so animated three days ago, now consists of only three women behind paltry stalls. I barely have time to pay for my Snickers before the first mortar rounds fall some fifty feet away. "Well, this is it. Now it's our turn," I tell myself, as I hurry off.

But what should I do? Where should I go? I can't leave town now; it's too late. Besides, there's not a car on the roads.

As I jog towards Iakha's house, I remember that she lives very near the hospital, which the Russians will surely continue to target. But where else can I go? No one is left on the streets. The inhabitants have barricaded themselves in their houses against an approaching hurricane—a hurricane of steel.

The artillery fire is coming closer; planes have just appeared overhead. I cover the remaining feet in a run. The villagers have all disappeared into their cellars. I burst into Iaskha's only to discover that she has no cellar; and now it's too late to cross the street and take refuge with the neighbors. "In any case, cellar or no cellar," Iakha sighs, "if the bomb makes a direct hit, nothing will protect you. When it comes down to it, cellars are useless."

I have to agree. Cellars are more of a psychological support than anything else. And so there we are, the five of us: Iakha, Vakha, Anzor, a young man from the village, and I; each of us sits in a chair or on the edge of the sofa—and waits.

The bombing is horrific. First, the windowpanes are blown to smithereens. Burning bits of steel tear through the air. The walls tremble. The doors fly open. During the attack, Iakha goes imperturbably about her household tasks, sweeping up the splintered window glass, putting the kettle on for tea.

Iakha's grandmother is lying against the wall in an adjoining room. I know that the old woman is a little deaf, but she must hear what's going on outside. During a moment's pause, she shouts out suddenly, "Is there anyone still alive?" Her voice is hoarse and tense. Iakha rushes to her side, takes her hand, and explains that we are all still here. I join her, and I, too, grip the old woman's bony forearm. I need this human contact desperately. Iakha has told me about the time she went down into a neighbor's cellar with her grandmother during the previous war. All the others crowded around the old woman. Superstition has it that a woman's great age will protect her and those around her from death. I don't believe in this sort of magic, but right now I have no other hope. The old lady begins to recite her prayers, and I, too, mumble some awkward pleas. When the bombs fall, everyone prays.

A powerful blast blows me right off the sofa where I was sitting, bolt upright, cottonmouthed, staring vacantly into space. Near the stove, I discover that the floor is warm. I decide to stay there on the ground. It's all the same, really. I contemplate my black skirt spread out around my drawn-up legs like the petals of a flower. Then I realize that, in a direct hit, I would be the first to be burnt alive. The stove's metal shards would go straight through me. But the yellow glow of the fire calms me, and I stay there, preferring the proximity of heat to my cold spot on the sofa.

We speak little. Everyone is alone with his or her thoughts. No shouting, no crying. Young Anzor strikes matches and smokes. Vakha is unmoving, with one hand held over his heart. Iakha is the most natural. I admire her: She sits there calmly, with her rosy cheeks, her dimples just ready to break out in a sweet smile, her ample bosom rising and falling with each steady breath. A hundred times I ask her, mechanically, if it will all be over soon and the planes will go away—all questions to which she, like me, does not know the answer. A hundred times she reassures me, sweetly, that, yes, it will all be over soon, that everything will be fine in just a little while. And a hundred times I believe what she says, at least for a few seconds, before I ask the same question all over again.

The nightmare will last more than four hours. The dive-bombing of the planes is deafening; the metallic slam of the shells incessant. Vakha consults his watch: "They're no doubt going to fire until nightfall." It's only two in the afternoon. Still hundreds of occasions to die before dusk.

Twice, in answer to the pressing calls of nature, no doubt provoked by my fear, I have to gather my courage and go outside. Outside into the war. The sky is orange. Black columns of smoke rise from almost every house. I know I'm in danger, but not more so than inside the house. Sitting on the sofa, "protected" by four walls, is just like sitting in a chair in the middle of the courtyard. Nothing can withstand the powerful fire of the Russian planes. But here I am participating in the spectacle, acting out my own fate. I can see the planes clearly as they drop their deadly cargo. As I go inside and close the door behind me, I have no illusions of safety. I am ridiculously, painfully small.

At nightfall, around five o'clock, three *boyviki* carrying a wounded man on a stretcher appear in our courtyard. As Vakha had predicted, the planes have gone away; now the only sound is that of firing artillery. We all rise when the soldiers kick open our front door to make room for the stretcher. They drop the bloodied human form like a bundle of dirty laundry on the yellow velvet sofa.

Mussa, a twenty-two-year-old Wahhabi fighter who left Grozny this morning has lost his left foot in a mine explosion. The hospital is full. There is absolutely no more space for the wounded, so the *boyviki* are dispersing them in private houses. They will pick Mussa up later. After twenty minutes, a nurse appears. "A Wahhabi," Iakha whispers to me discretely, pointing to her scarf, which is fastened tightly around her neck with a nurse's pin. Out of her leather bag the nurse quickly extracts syringes, painkillers, and tranquilizers.

Iakha struggles to hide her unhappiness; she cannot risk angering the Wahhabis by refusing to help. And because she also feels sorry for this wounded young combatant, she gives in.

The grandmother, who is more attentive to the noises around her than we imagine, calls Iakha to her bedside to ask her a question that's been troubling her: Russians would not, by any chance, have entered the house? If so, we must kick them out. "As long as I live, I won't tolerate one here!" she exclaims. I kneel down by her bedside. Feeling my presence, she searches for my hand. Her thin fingers press against mine. With Iakha's help, I ask her if she remembers any period of her life without a Russian presence in her country. "Yes," she says, assuredly. "It was when I was twenty." Looking at her skeletal, wrinkled face in the shadows, I think I see her smile.*

Iakha sets the table for dinner as if nothing were wrong. Three more times everything begins to shake. Still, Iakha insists that we

---

* In May, a long letter from Iakha reached me in Moscow, informing me that her grandmother had died peacefully in her bed.

all sit down and eat. Two neighbors who have stopped by to check on us stay for supper, as well as two other neighbors who are taking refuge with us for the night. We eat burnt bread with our bowls of potato soup. No one has much of an appetite, but we force ourselves to eat. From outside in the dark streets comes the sound of automatic fire. "What are they doing now? Can't the rebels finally leave?" Iakha asks. The Russian troops respond with shells.

We stay up all night talking, to keep the fear from gnawing at our insides. The shooting continues, shaking the walls and our faked calm, the kind that one instinctively adopts to get a grip on one's fear. Nine of us huddle in the little room. Mussa lets out loud sighs and groans; he is suffering terribly but is trying not to let it show. Larissa nurses him. Several times, in my half-sleep, I see her large hands lift his head and help him drink. I also see the indefatigable Iakha in profile, bent over a tub, energetically brushing something that looks like a pair of trousers. The next morning I ask her whether I have dreamed this. No, she washed Anzor's jeans during the night. Despite the circumstances that have brought us all together here, I suspect that she is enjoying this closed little world in which she is at the center of everyone's needs. She concedes that she's happy to be useful. "I'm not afraid of death, I'm used to it," she says, her tone matter-of-fact. "If it comes, it comes."

The villagers venture from their cellars at dawn, their arms full of mattresses and blankets. I go outside for the first time in twenty-four hours and discover that our house has been saved by a miracle. All around us, the village is steeped in blood and ruins. On all sides, the houses have been razed. Everywhere is smoking debris and dust. The sight is devastating.

Around the hospital, nothing is left standing. Almost every private house within a radius of fifty yards has been reduced to rubble. Bodies are strewn about the streets, frozen stiff, in the positions they died in. The hospital's white walls are riddled with shell holes. Inside, the rooms are topsy-turvy, the corridors awash in blood. Groups of men are wandering from one room to another, trying to recover medicines, weapons, and clothing. A sickening odor wafts about with each gust of wind; they're burning clothing and pieces of arms and legs cut off in yesterday's amputations.

I remembered to bring my camera with me, and I use it for the first time in this war. I photograph what I see around me in the hospital: *Boyviki* killed as they fled Grozny and left here on mattresses during the attack. In another room, I recognize the face of a young fighter who arrived on Monday, January 31, with the first group. He had stepped on a mine and his leg was amputated that day. Yesterday, he told me all about his hatred for the Russians; today he is frozen in death.

Yesterday, the surgeon Khassan Baiev performed more than sixty amputations on combatants and civilians. Today, all that's left on the blood-soaked operating table is some dirty linen and one grisly tool: An electric saw.

In the back yard of a house across the street from the hospital, where I had spent several hours in conversation with Khamzat, the

Bamut commander, lies the rigid body of a *boyvik* killed by a
bomb as he ran to take shelter in a barn. According to the survivors of this house, he was a Russian who had converted to Islam,
which explains his green Islamic headband.

A little farther away, in the icy alleyway behind the hospital, I
find another body on an improvised sled. Usually, the rebels take
their dead with them so that they can be buried in their native villages, but this body had to be abandoned when the bombing
began. Another corpse, a civilian who was caught outside when a
ground-to-ground missile struck his house, has been covered with
a white sheet by a neighbor. His flashlight lies in the snow by his
side, still faintly illuminating the gory scene.

Nearby, a young woman is kneeling and weeping beside the
remains of her rebel brothers. One of the bodies is rolled in a sheet
and tied at the neck and the ankles, signifying that the individual
was dead when he arrived in the village. The others died during
last night's bombardment.

I come across some traumatized children. They don't seem to
know how to behave in the presence of dead bodies. Two of them,
wrapped up against the cold, have come running from the house
next door. They are looking on gravely and quietly, assessing the
damage their neighbors have suffered.

An ashen woman contemplates the debris piled in her courtyard. Like the others, she is terrorized, both by the rebels, over
whom no one has any control, and by the Russians, who haven't
hesitated to attack, knowing that numerous civilian casualties
would result. The personal effects strewn about everywhere show
how quickly the *boyviki* fled the village once the shelling began.

Coming round a corner, I catch sight of the ample figure of Iakha. She's running with difficulty. My first impulse is to call out to her, but Vakha restrains me. We catch up to her silently. "Mussa must leave right away. We've got to find him civilian clothes, but I don't have any socks for him, and I can't find any anywhere." She is red-faced and out of breath and seems more frightened than yesterday, when the bombs were falling. It's my turn now to reassure her: "Rummage around in my plastic bag. I have two pairs in there, wool ones. They'll fit him." Iakha thanks me and runs off toward the house.

During yesterday's attack, some fifty villagers have been killed; their families are now burying them hastily in their gardens. They would be too much of a target if they dared to take the bodies to the town cemetery, at the entrance to the village.

⌒

The inhabitants of Alkhan Kala cannot yet recover their peace of mind. Now the village must live in fear of the *zachistka*. They are worried that Russian soldiers will search their houses while the *boyviki* are still there

Three buses flying white flags are parked near the hospital; a small crowd is gathered around them. I recognize the proud figure of Umar Khanbiev, the rebel Minister of Health. He spreads his arms wide in a gesture of welcome when he sees me. He explains that he left Grozny the previous day with the second group. His face is lined and his features drawn, but he is calm: "What I witnessed yesterday, as we left Grozny, is indescribable. Never in my poor life as a Chechen fighting for my freedom have I seen such things. I don't know how I was able to get my fifteen doctors and nurses out, but, thankfully, not one of us was injured."

Umar is trying to move the dozens of wounded and dying rebel fighters to another hospital, most likely in Urus-Martan. To do this, they will have to pass through the Russian zone. They must negotiate with the enemy for their safe transit; payment will be made in cash.

Mussa, the soldier who stayed at Iakha's house, is now shaved, bathed, and dressed as a civilian, so that he can take part in the convoy. A collection has been gathered to pay for the passage of the vehicles through the Russian barricades. "The soldiers would sell their mothers for vodka," Anzor assures Mussa, as he escorts him to the hospital.

Calm has once again settled over Iakha's house. I find Iakha seated at the kitchen table, peeling potatoes. Vakha is snoozing on the sofa. He's been telling me for the last three days that we must leave here as soon as possible. Yes, but how? We are surrounded by Federal forces and have no means of transport. For now, we must wait, wait for the situation to evolve, for an opportunity....

The most immediate threat is the Russians, who have appeared in the village for one of their "cleansing" operations. They work fairly methodically, going from one house to the next, street after street. Our sources tell us that they are, at the moment, not far from the market. "We have at least an hour," Iakha declares. Once again, she is not at all shaken by the prospect of imminent danger. Until now, I have avoided *zachistki* at all costs, for fear of being discovered. This time, I have no alternative and no place to hide. The Russians will search everywhere.

"Lie down on the sofa and try to look ill," Iakha says simply. "At least that way you won't have to talk. I'll tell them that you're a cousin from Samashkii who's come to visit me, and that you couldn't leave because of what's happened. You have a fever. I'm looking after you as well as my paralyzed grandmother."

From experience—the Federals have already come to inspect the village on several occasions—Iakha knows that they'll balk at searching about in the dark room of the old woman. "She frightens them," she assures me. And so we plant all my equipment— the camera, notebooks, and the satellite telephone—under the frail legs of the old woman.

Then we wait. I roll myself in a blanket and stretch out, following Iakha's instructions. I have no trouble feigning illness. I feel Vakha looking at me from his place on the sofa. I don't know if he approves of our little drama, but he hasn't proposed anything better. Iakha has gone back to peeling potatoes slowly. She wants to be occupied with some very banal task when the Russians burst in on us. She doesn't take her eyes off the gate that opens onto the courtyard.

Little by little, the voices get louder, their words more distinct. I listen hard: Yes, they're speaking in Russian. They can't be far off now. "Two houses away," Iakha whispers, taking her work even more slowly. Now I'm beginning to feel sick in earnest. I open my eyes and close them again; I'm too hot; I don't know what position to put myself in. I have the impression that everything about me suggests I'm a foreigner who's broken in like a criminal on the Chechen scene. Now the sound of voices is very close by. I hear the crunch of heavy steps on gravel. I close my eyes, expecting at any moment to hear Iakha greet the soldiers in Russian. But nothing. We continue to wait, still playing our roles. Vakha remains silent, his eyes half-closed. Maybe he's even gone to sleep.

After fifteen minutes—an eternity, it seems—Iakha gets up and crosses the courtyard to look in the street. A few minutes later, she runs back, her pale face broken into a broad smile. "They've gone, can you believe it? They passed right in front of the house without coming in, even though all the other houses in the street were checked. Incredible!"

She rushes back to her vegetables and finishes the job in the wink of an eye. Vakha jumps to his feet and pulls on his overcoat. I throw off the heavy covers and sit up on the edge of the sofa.

"Another miracle," I say to myself. "Now we'll finally be able to leave."

⌂

As we would learn later in the afternoon, two streets away from ours, the Russians, for no particular reason, summarily executed seven persons, including two women. Rumor has it that the soldiers were blind drunk.

Chapter 7

I t's Thursday morning. Thanks to Saittami and his knowledge of the highways and byways around Alkhan Kala, we are
able to leave the village. Vakha is coming with me; Larissa will stay
behind.

We put on fisherman's boots to cross a river, and suddenly we
find ourselves in another village, this one untouched by the recent
bombardments.

There, we find a car, then another, and still another, and at last
we arrive safe and sound in Novye Atagi. As we turn into the
courtyard at Anzor Dzhivrolibov's, I rush ahead, happy to be
returning to this family who welcomed me so warmly in the past.
They must have been worried when Vakha didn't come back; they
probably don't know that we were in the middle of the attack on
Alkhan Kala. I see the silhouette of Elena, sweeping the courtyard
in the morning's faint light; we throw ourselves into each other's

arms. I rush to greet her sister, the girls, and Anzor, who's already at work in his office in the other wing of the house. They seem relieved to have me back again.

I treat myself to a thorough wash, pouring bucket after bucket of warm water over my head in the bathroom, which still does not have running water. Then I eat. Indeed, I spend the day eating. I am unable to stop. I am worn out, and feel as if a heavy stone were dragging me to the bottom of deep water. It's not a disagreeable sensation.

This evening, reflecting on the horrific events of the last few days, I suddenly remember what the rebels told me in the midst of the panic in the hospital: "Yes, we bought our way out of Grozny, but it cost us more than we had thought, and not just in human lives." The pro-independence fighters in Alkhan Kala didn't try to hide the fact that "everything in this war has a price," including the passage through enemy lines. And, for once, the information put out by both camps agrees; I learn later that Vladimir Shamanov, a Russian general, declared on Russian television that the "terrorists" had paid $100,000 to buy their way out of the capital. The Russians congratulated themselves on the success of this special operation, which they called "Wolf Hunt." The many civilian casualties were just another figure in their profits and losses ledger.

How do the two enemies manage to meet and exchange money on a field during war? "It's very simple," one of the combatants told me. "You pick special emissaries for the exchange, and the money passes in cash from the Chechen side to the Russians. It's given to the officers, not to the simple soldiers."

It appeared, moreover, that the Russians had anticipated the *boyviki* departure from Grozny at least four days before it happened. We were circling around the capital at the time. It occurs to me now that the troops at the checkpoints had been considerably reinforced, with more soldiers than usual stationed at the entrances and exits to Shaly, Argun, Novye Atagi, and Urus-Martan. Russian tanks were positioned in freshly dug trenches; soldiers scrupulously checked every male under sixty, and even verified the papers of women—an unusual occurrence.

There is another version of the Alkhan Kala corridor story. Many Chechens refuse to believe that the *boyviki* paid to leave their positions; they believe that the initiative came from the Federals, who bribed certain Chechen commanders to persuade their troops to leave the city. These commanders accepted because they believed that they could retake Grozny once the Russians occupied it.

In both versions of the events, the Russian corridor was nothing more than a trap. Everyone agrees on that.

In this war, money plays an important role not only for the combatants but also for the thousands of civilians who are the unwitting victims of the battles. Russian officers and soldiers traffic in anything that falls into their hands. And many Chechens believe that certain elements in the rebel command "make money" by waging war "on the backs of the people."

During my absence, while Starye Atagi was being "cleansed"

by the troops of the Russian Ministry of the Interior, fifty-four persons, men and women, were carried off without explanation. These arbitrary arrests were like kidnappings; several days after the disappearances, the families were informed through a complex system of intermediaries that their relatives would be returned in exchange for 1,000 rubles [about $40] per hostage. The leaders of the racket, who are not necessarily at the top of the military hierarchy, make a tidy profit. As I drove back from Alkhan Kala, this was the sole topic of conversation among my fellow passengers. "I finally got my nephew back, six days after he disappeared, in exchange for three automatic weapons," one man explained. "Oh, yes? I've come myself to try to get my two sons, who disappeared during a Russian identity check not far from here," a woman answered. The man turned to her sympathetically: "Then I'd advise you to make contact with 'X,' who'll take you to 'Y.' He'll help you recover your sons for money or valuables."

The bodies of the *boyviki* and of the enemy wounded are also pawns in serious financial discussions with the Russians. The cadaver of the rebel commander Lechi Dudayev, who was killed by a mine as he was leaving Grozny with the first group of fighters, is said to have been dug up already by the Federals; they plan to resell his body to his family.

⌂

One evening at Anzor's, I am sitting in the kitchen drinking tea with the women when a neighbor appears in the living room. He's accompanied by a bearded man in uniform. Elena, like a good hostess, speaks to them in Chechen and offers them tea and cookies. The uniformed man answers in Russian, almost apologetically, for he is, it turns out, a Russian soldier. None of us knows quite how to react. What's he doing here? Why has the neighbor brought him into the house? Does Anzor know what's going on?

"Don't worry, he's a friend," Akhmed, the neighbor, reassures us. "I have a matter to settle with him and his group before he returns to his garrison at Chiri Yurt."

Confidence established, Piotr, the Russian, goes out to the courtyard and brings in yet another man, Igor, who's thoroughly chilled by his wait. They sit down at the table, light cigarettes, and eagerly help themselves to the biscuits offered by Elena and her sister.

The two Russians have blue eyes, high cheekbones, crewcut hair, and the gift of gab. They come from Vladivostock,* the capital of the Russian Far East. Piotr is the commander of the SOBR brigade, which has been stationed in Chiri Yurt since the end of November. Igor, a large fellow, bald as a cue ball, is his *zam*.† They are disgusted with this war. As far as they're concerned, it has nothing to do with any sort of independence movement.

"This time, there's not one *boyvik* who knows why he's fighting. I defy anyone to find me a Chechen fighter who talks about independence for his country! The reasons for this war are entirely different," Piotr explains. He has a degree from the FSB academy, and is clearly delighted to pontificate before a foreign journalist.

---

* Located fifteen time zones away from Chechnya.
† Right arm, in Russian.

Igor, who's just as eager to talk, breaks in: "This war is just a sordid tale of money-grubbing. Everybody knows that. And we shouldn't have anything to do with this so-called Operation Antiterrorist. It's a total farce."

"It's a real war, and an expensive one, of course," Piotr elaborates. "That much we know. After all, we live it on a daily basis. And we also know that the Chechen population is the first victim of this nightmare. Here people are dying so that others can line their pockets with money. It's just disgusting!" He lets his spoon fall loudly into his cup of hot tea.

I ask the Russians why the SOBR battalion is stationed here. "To make sure that everything is going smoothly in the territories under our control, the 'liberated territories,'" Piotr answers sarcastically. I press him further, asking whether, in case of a surprise rebel attack, their troops are supposed to intervene to protect the lives of the peaceful villagers. "Not at all. We are not prepared for that kind of operation, even though we can't exclude the possibility that the *boyviki* might reappear as an even more powerful menace," the officer explains impassively. "Our priorities are the control posts at the entrances and exits of the villages. Everything else is theoretically the province of the army."

For these two servants of the Russian state—who are paid about $165 a month—the causes of their discontent are much more profound than this disagreeable Chechen situation. "Ever since the end of the USSR, nothing works anymore," Igor observes. He draws deeply on his cigarette. "We are supposed to serve a state that no longer exists. We can't relate to any head of the government, not even Putin, who has yet to prove himself. He has a certain weight, sure, but there must be someone else behind him pulling the strings. We do only one thing—obey orders. What Russia really needs is a dictator who will restore order. Such a person must exist somewhere, but we haven't found him yet. Pity!"

Their hearts aren't in this war. Neither Piotr nor Igor knows why he's in Chechnya. "Our presence here serves absolutely no purpose," Piotr says. "This war is useless, and all the officers we know feel the same way, without exception! Whether there are peace talks or not, the war will eventually end. But the problems will remain unresolved. It's this almost certainty of the uselessness of our actions that is so destructive for morale," he assures me.

Despite everything they say, the two men are serious professionals. At their base in Chiri Yurt, order reigns. Since the SOBR installed their headquarters in the local kindergarten, not one *boyvik* has appeared, not even in civilian "disguise." Nor has one automatic weapon been heard in the village. The Russians have the complete cooperation of the residents. Teams appointed and led by the Chechen head of the village administration—someone was appointed to this post well before the war began—patrol the perimeter of the kindergarten to thwart provocative acts. In this way, the battalion is protected. "We protect them during the day, and they do the same for us at night," Piotr explains. "After the departure of the Russian troops from Chechnya—because we will have to leave one of these days—there will be civil war for two or three years. It's inevitable. It will be the same capitulation; the same pseudo-accords; and once again it will be the civilian population who will suffer."

When Anzor appears, all three rise and exchange the usual

courtesies. Clearly, they know each other, but Anzor looks furious; he contains his anger only with great difficulty. As soon as the Russians leave, he thunders, "Who let them in?"

"Akhmed brought them. I thought it was with your consent." Elena, looking grief-stricken, tries to defend herself.

"But don't you understand, they're going to turn us in, they're going to sell us! We're finished!" he thunders.

A little later, I look for Anzor in the office to try to clarify the situation. We agree that it would be better if I left the next day.

Chapter 8

I WAKE EARLY, get up, and head to the kitchen, where I find Elena. She looks glum.

"I can't take any more of this war," she tells me. "Just look at the way we're living, shut in like prisoners! As soon as it all began, in October, I told Anzor that we should get out of here. But he said it was our duty to stay; the village was watching us. They were all waiting for us to go, precisely because we had the means to do it. But no, we were going to stay. We were going to show the Russians we're not afraid of them. Well, I've had enough. Time is passing, my own best years are behind me, and I see no future at all for my daughters."

She leaves to draw water from the cistern next to the garage. "Put the water on to boil. We'll have breakfast together; that way we can at least chat a little in peace," she adds, as she disappears down the hall.

I strike a match and turn on the gas. As I turn to put the box of matches back beside the refrigerator, a movement outside catches my eye. Shadowy figures are crossing the courtyard. I draw closer to the kitchen window. Now I can make out the shapes of fifteen or so camouflaged figures in black hoods; they have ammunition belts across their chests, and their fingers are poised on the triggers of their Kalachnikovs.

"Where is the man of the house?" a voice shouts in Russian, breaking the frosty calm of the early morning. Everything is happening so quickly that I hardly have time to think. I know that these men have come hunting for me, that I am the sole reason for this invasion. I hope desperately that this episode will be over quickly. I can't let anything happen to Anzor's family.

I rush into the bedroom. The household is sleeping. I must wake them up. "Russians are in the courtyard," I tell Tabarka brusquely. She has time only to pull her tights on under her skirt. Since the start of the war, the Chechens have all slept in their clothes in case they have to run for cover at a moment's notice. It takes Tabarka two seconds to get fully dressed.

The Russians have already entered. Five of them occupy the women's wing of the house. I am pacing about in the bedroom. The girls have begun to whimper. Tabarka, staring dumbfounded, runs a comb through her hair. I am wondering where Elena and Anzor are, how they are taking this. The masked men immediately set about searching the most remote corners of the house. One of them barks a warning at us, as though speaking to children: "Let's get this straight right from the start. You have nothing to worry about if you don't move and stay right here in this room." Tabarka nods vaguely. I say nothing. I try to gather my wits and decide that I must find their leader and explain my situation before they take me away. But no one seems to be the least bit interested in us or our identities; they are behaving almost as if we didn't exist.

I curb my desire to watch what they are doing, especially with my personal affairs, which are spread out on the table in the living room, where I spent the night. I am sure they're going to find my satellite phone, my articles written in longhand, and, tucked away in one of my blouses, my working notes, my address book, my French passport, my Russian visa, and my official press pass identifying me as a foreign correspondent authorized to work within the territory of the Russian Federation.

Through the cloudy glass of the bedroom door, I watch an enormous shadow receding. It's a man carrying a bulky instrument with cords dangling from it: My satellite telephone. About twenty-five minutes later, when the officers are distracted, I sneak out of the bedroom along with two of Anzor's girls. In the living room, everything is topsy-turvy—the carpet is peeled back, the wall covering is wrenched away, sofas are ripped open. I rush to the plastic bag that holds my personal effects to see if the little pouch with my identity papers is still inside. If they've taken it, I won't be able to prove my identity or my status. With relief I discover that the papers are still there.

I need to know what's happening in the courtyard, where Anzor, dressed in his overcoat, is waiting patiently as an FSB inspector fills boxes with confiscated goods. The Russians have amassed hundreds of videocassettes—Anzor's precious personal documentaries—a heap of papers, and, among other bric-a-brac, a

sticker bearing the colors of independent "Ichkeria." I catch sight
of my telephone in a box a little to one side.

I make my way toward the inspector, who looks out of sorts, as
if his mission has been unfruitful, and speak to him in Russian: "I
am the French journalist; those are my things there, in the carton.
I am ready to answer any of your questions."

He continues his work without looking up, pausing only to
growl, with a gesture of dismissal, "Get out of here."

I don't know what to do. Anzor, who has observed my attempt
to intervene, also appears to wish that I would shut up and keep
my distance. Perhaps he wants to show goodwill to the FSB, or
maybe he has understood something here that has escaped me. I
thought they were coming for me, but I am quite wrong. Eventually, they leave with Anzor in their jeep, followed by an army
truck. The women promptly burst into tears. I am confused. How
could the FSB "forget" to interrogate an individual who confesses
to being a journalist and therefore a certified troublemaker?

As soon as the Russians are gone, the inhabitants of the village
begin to arrive in a steady stream. It is the custom for all—close
friends as well as distant acquaintances—to parade their sorrow
before the family in a gesture of solidarity. The women, who are
crowding outside the doors of the house, feel obliged to weep
loudly, as if Anzor were dead.

"If they didn't, I could—so the custom goes—hold it against
them that they didn't grieve enough," Elena whispers to me. She
assumes the role of the pitiful wife stoically, but is not taken in by
all this play-acting. "I just hope they don't beat him. His health is
so fragile"; this is all she says on the subject of her husband.

I am congratulating myself that Islam, my travel companion, was absent during the morning's events, for the Russians would certainly have taken him away, too. All day long, I mull over what has happened, coming gradually to the realization that the raid was conceived and planned long ago and has nothing to do with me.

The Russians have left behind an official report of their search, which I do my best to decipher. It's the second carbon copy of a hand-written document, and it isn't easy going. At last I make it out with the help of Ibragim, one of Anzor's brothers, who has stood guard outside the house since Anzor's forced departure. We learn the official purpose of the search: Anzor is accused of hiding a television relay station in the walls of his house and broadcasting the pro-independence channel "Ichkeria."

"But you're not going to find a television antenna hidden in books," Ibragim remarks, referring to the hundreds of volumes in his brother's library, which has just been methodically sacked.

That evening, Islam reappears. He already knows about the search mission; the news has made the tour of the surrounding villages. He is upset and unhappy and insists that I leave with him immediately. "You don't understand," he says. "They could come back from one moment to the next, tonight even, to take you away. You have no grasp of the situation. The Russians are to be avoided at all costs. Follow me!"

But for the first time since we met and he began to help me, I stand up to him. I don't agree with Islam at all; on the contrary, I know it is my duty to stay here within these walls and to wait for the Russians to bring everything back.

"They didn't come for me. They didn't even pay any attention to me," I try to convince Islam. "The problem now is that they know I exist, and I can no longer avoid confronting them."

Finally, bone-tired and discouraged, I lose patience and begin to cry, because, in truth, I yearn to follow Islam, who would certainly find a way to get us out to Ingushetia. Still, something tells me that I would be wrong to leave—and I need to get my phone and notes back. I am also annoyed that the FSB found me without even trying. I need a final "confrontation" with the Russians.

Days pass: Tuesday, Wednesday, Thursday. The waiting is interminable. I need to send a message back to the Moscow bureau to let them know that I am alive and well, but I'm stuck without my phone. Tempted in spite of myself by Islam, who renews his campaign every morning, I am continually struggling with the same questions. Should I leave or stay? If I leave, they Russians will come after me, and it will look as if I ran away. If I stay, I'll waste time and also serve as a target for certain village bad-mouthers who are already attacking me for having brought trouble. Fortunately, Elena pays no attention to these silly gossips. At last, I decide to stay because I must get my stuff back, if only to continue working. I will wait for Anzor. Legally he cannot be held more than seventy-two hours.

On Thursday morning, Anzor is still not back. At that moment, I decide to write a letter in Russian explaining my situation. I will entrust the letter to Islam, who will read it over the telephone to the bureau. But how will we find a phone? All the lines in Chechnya were cut at the beginning of the war. I heard a week ago that a line had possibly been opened in Urus-Martan, now under Russian control. I beg Islam to stop there on his way to Ingushetia; but I know it will be difficult for him to move about because the Russians are opening and closing roads and check-points randomly and cracking down on "locals"—especially young men. I fold the letter and place it carefully in his shirt pocket.

"Consider it done," he tells me before he disappears.

I am reassured and worried at the same time. If Islam doesn't come back in time for our departure on Saturday night, and if, in the meantime, Anzor hasn't reappeared, I will have to leave on my own. The uncertainty has lasted long enough. My nerves are stretched as tight as a drum.

Days later, when I'm back in Moscow, I will finally be able to reach Islam by telephone. He will explain to me, in dramatic tones, how he succeeded in "passing the message." As it happened, a telephone line was open in Urus-Martan, but it was located in the *kommandantura*. Without hesitating, Islam stood in a long line—composed almost entirely of women—which zigzagged out-side and into the street. He waited patiently, with downcast eyes, trying to look as "normal" as possible, while Russian soldiers milled about. He waited close to two hours. Finally, as he neared one of the two working phones, he realized there was no light in the telephone booth. How was he going to read my message? He felt around in his pockets for a matchbox. Only by striking match after match—he used up the entire box—could he see to repeat my text to the Moscow representative of *Libération*, who jotted it down as he dictated. The connection was terrible, but Islam didn't dare raise his voice.

The next evening, at dusk, neighbors come running to Elena's. They tell us they have heard extracts from my letter on Radio Svoboda. What a relief! The Moscow bureau must be in a state, I tell myself, but at least they know that I am still alive.

Saturday morning, while I am doing my chores—in my idleness, I have evolved from a journalist into a model Chechen housewife—washing dishes, peeling potatoes, sweeping the rugs with my reed broom—I find myself face to face with armed men again. It takes me several seconds to realize that Anzor is back, safe and sound.

The prosecutor's assistant who questioned Anzor at Mozdok has released him for lack of evidence. The FBS inspector who directed Monday's search operation has come back, too, but this time he is more accommodating.

"It's Anne, isn't it?" he asks. "I'm so glad to see you. Could we have a little talk?"

"You know, I'm happy to see you again, too," I reply gaily. "You've taken your sweet time in getting around to this conversation, even though I certainly wasn't hard to find. You've cost me a week! And what would you have done, if you'd come back to Anzor's and found me gone?"

The tone is bantering, but I am wary, all the same.

"We would have begun a search for you," he answers drily.

A few glances exchanged with Anzor and I know that everything is all right. But I can't talk things over with him until the Russians leave. The FSB inspector, accompanied by a colleague and another man from the prosecutor's office, wants to look over my papers. I go into the house to fetch them and rejoin the Russians in the *banya*.* They are sitting there, smoking, looking slyly amused.

"So you're a journalist? That's not a lie, after all? Well, what are you doing here all by yourself, huh? You wouldn't be a spy, would you?" one of them asks as an opening gambit.

I can't be sure whether they're serious, and set about to convince them that I am a real journalist, based in Russia, which I've been covering for more than a year.

"Yes, but illegally," insists the same man, whose name, I will later learn, is Arkadi.

"Illegally, in your eyes, but not in mine," I answer coolly.

"How have you been travelling in this zone without being noticed?"

Here I can hardly hold back a smile. "Why don't you ask the soldiers in charge of the checkpoints? I've been here for five months, and not once has anyone asked to see my papers."

They exchange looks, silent, perplexed.

"Good. You'll come along with us?" the inspector asks.

"Where, exactly?"

"To Mozdok."

I think fast. In the first place, I don't really have any choice, and, if what they're saying is true, going with them will spare me the hardship of traveling the same route on my own. In a sense, it's an easy way out. They assure me that my things are now in Moz-

---

* A Russian version of the sauna.

dok, and that I will be able to recover them if I cooperate. I accept their offer; before leaving, however, I write a note to Islam so that he will have something to go on if I disappear: "At 12:30 this morning, Saturday, February 11, I agreed to leave Novye Atagi with two inspectors of the FSB and one inspector from the prosecutor's office. Our destination, according to them, is Mozdok."

As I leave, I embrace Elena and slip her the note.

△

We climb into an army vehicle. I take a seat in the rear, between the two intelligence officers, my black plastic bag resting on my knees. We speed across the Chechen territory, scarcely pausing at the frequent checkpoints. I wonder where Islam is at this moment, whether he has reached Ingushetia or will instead come back to fetch me this evening at Anzor's.

The car is traveling at a steady speed of about sixty-five miles an hour—"so that the bandits' snipers can't get us," one of my guards explains. I offer no reply, but this maneuver seems ridiculous to me. I know that if the *boyviki* decide to set up an ambush, no car would escape them. My traveling companions are right to be afraid. As the violet dusk settles, I sense the tension in their silence.

Mozdok is a long way. I try to avoid a possible interrogation by chattering. The judicial inspector suddenly interrupts my babble: "Do you know how to use a gun?" he asks. He indicates with his chin the Kalachnikov in his lap.

Taken aback, I stutter out that I don't, of course, but then I add, "The only time I ever fired a gun was in Russia. Yes, in a shooting club outside Moscow. Perhaps you know it?" No reaction. The subject is closed for now.

We carry on, heading north. Thirty minutes later, night is almost upon us, and we are crossing open country deep in the territory north of the River Terek with no control post in sight. Arkadi, seated on my right, rephrases the question: "Of course, your Chechen friends must have taught you to shoot, didn't they?"

I am surprised, but manage an answer: "My friends, as you call them, aren't really friends; they're people I meet in the course of my work. And when I meet them, it's not for shooting lessons; it's to take down their eyewitness accounts."

Are they playing with me? Testing me? I have no idea, but the inspector adds, "Then you don't know how to shoot. Well, we'll just see about that." He turns toward the chauffeur, who has already begun to slow down, and says, "Let's stop here. It's a good spot. Nobody around."

Nobody around? I clasp the handles of my plastic bag more tightly. I can't believe that they're really going to make me get out of the car and … then what? Will they put a Kalashnikov in my hands and wait for me to use it? Would they run such a risk? Could this be the purpose of the operation? Will they jump me as soon as we're out of the car? Or are they just playing with me? All four of them are looking at me, waiting. I don't move a muscle. The inspector begins again, but without conviction: "You're really sure that you don't know how to shoot? You wouldn't even be curious to try?"

I feel my head shaking no, and I add, for emphasis, "No.

Thank you, but no. I really have no desire to try it. Really, not in the least."

He turns and makes a sign to the driver. The car continues on its way.

I relax a little as we cross the frontier into North Ossetia, where Mozdok is located. We drive straight to a hotel. They confiscate my press pass and identity papers "so that I won't disappear."

"Of course, you won't leave the hotel," they add, after escorting me to the door of my room. We agree to meet the next morning at nine o'clock.

The hotel is full of armed soldiers and carefully made-up young women. The room is simple in the extreme: A bunk, a wash basin, a lamp, and a blanket. I would love to throw myself on the bed and sleep, but first I must find a telephone. I pay no attention to the officers' order, and slip out of my room.

I have just stopped an old woman in the street when I hear a familiar voice calling my name. It's a photographer friend who is on his way to the hotel to have a drink with a colleague. He tells me that everyone in Moscow is worried sick about me. We go off in search of a telephone and find the post office open. Without a moment to lose, I dial the two numbers that I know by heart: The *Libération* bureau and the home of the bureau chief, Véronique Soulé. Busy, both of them! Because the FSB has taken my address book, I can't try other numbers. My friend digs about in his notes, and we dial the number of a mutual colleague in Moscow. He answers, asks me if I can "move about freely," and inquires about the state of my health. I reassure him that I'm fine.

The next day, at two minutes to nine, I meet my "host" from

the prosecutor's office, who is seated in an armchair in the hotel lobby. The prosecutor's office is nearby, and we go there on foot. The interrogation room has been freshly painted and the smell is overpowering.

They ask for my life's story, how and why I became a journalist, and about my travels in Chechnya. The inspector meeds details: How I'm travelling and with whom. I choose my words carefully. I make no mention of Islam or anyone else. The interrogation is polite. My questioner, whose humor seems to have improved since yesterday, is not shy about sharing his own thoughts on the current situation. His work is difficult, he confides, but he tries to do it conscientiously "as you do yours." He seems pleased to have found some common ground between us.

Around noon, they allow me to search through the boxes they have brought from Anzor's house, which are now lying in a messy heap in the room next door. I recover all the things that were confiscated from me. The inspector is intrigued by my satellite phone and asks me to show him how it works. I am delighted to do so, because it gives me a chance to call the Moscow bureau. Joyfully, I tell Véronique Soulé that everything is all right.

I have forgotten, however, that the two FSB officers will join us for the afternoon interrogation. This session is much less friendly. They ask me to go over the contents of my articles, indeed, practically to translate them word for word. One of the agents, Arkadi, sits opposite me. My notebook lies open between us on the table. He asks that we examine the contents page by page. I am careful to translate only the most banal passages, judiciously avoiding anything that might be of real interest to him. When we reach the last page, he closes the notebook. I hold out my hand to take it back, but he gets up and heads for the copy machine. He copies the entire notebook, and my manuscript articles as well, although I tell him that he could just as easily consult the *Libération* webiste, where everything has already been published.

Last, he jots down a few telephone numbers from my notebook. I sign a statement. The prosecutor's men are delighted, and so am I. They reprimand me only for having failed to register within three days of my arrival in Novye Atagi, as required by Russian law. The FSB guys, however, are grumbling that my press pass is not in order—but they don't really appear to know what they're talking about. As far as the prosecutor's office is concerned, the affair is closed. The inspector's "Thank you, Ma'am, have a good trip back to Moscow" fills me with relief. Again, the two henchmen from the FSB don't see things in the same light. "What are your plans now? What do you intend to do?" they want to know.

"Go home, of course," I respond.

They don't believe me. "Arkadi has nothing planned for tomorrow. He will be happy to accompany you to the nearest airport and put you on the first plane for Moscow. For your own security, of course," one of them says.

"I certainly don't need your protection!" I tell myself. But I know that I have no choice in the matter. I will have an escort whether I like it or not.

We've arranged for Arkadi to pick me up at ten o'clock to escort me to the airport in Ingushetia. Twenty minutes before the appointed hour, he pounds on the door of my hotel room.

"Why did you lie to me, Anne? The truth is, you write anti-Russian articles. You tricked us!" he barks accusingly.

I don't even bother to get up. Arkadi goes on with his monologue. Apparently, his FSB colleagues in Moscow spent the night researching my work on the Internet. The thought that Arkadi followed my advice brings a smile to my lips.

When I finally get up, Arkadi informs me that there is a further problem: The FSB have telephoned to say that they want the originals rather than the copies of my notes and articles. Here, I stop cold in my tracks. What on earth could this mean? If they are going to take my originals, I demand the photocopies in exchange. Arkadi is unsure what to do. After a moment of hesitation, he announces that he will "take the responsibility" upon himself, as if he were dealing with an affair of the very highest gravity. We set off for the prosecutor's office, where, at my suggestion, we put everything in writing.

The prosecutor's staff make jokes when we turn up again. The inspector who dealt with my case the previous day even offers advice to his colleague in "the agency" on the proper wording of the necessary document. Arkadi works for twenty minutes, laboriously copying out legalistic formulations from a law textbook. In the meantime, the prosecutor's inspector follows me into the hall and tells me confidentially that "this isn't very legal, but it's very much in the style of the FSB." He shrugs his shoulders and disappears. Although the FSB would no doubt have preferred that our "exchange" leave no trace, I have their promise, in a crudely drawn-up, hand-written document, to return my original papers before May 1, 2000.* They put me on the next plane for Moscow.

This encounter with the Russian forces of order, the last chapter in my six-month odyssey in Chechnya, has been, all things considered, rather comic. It brings a temporary halt to my investigation of this tragic and brutal war.

---

* As of December 2000, I have yet to receive a document.

Epilogue

I WROTE THIS BOOK after my interrogation and deportation by the FSB in February 2000. Since then, I returned to the Chechen republic on two occasions. First in August, when I traveled for three days as a guest of the Russian Army (to demonstrate my good will to the Russians, who seemed to regard me with a great deal of curiosity), then in September and October, when I went alone. Once again I witnessed the war from the Chechen side, where I had complete freedom of movement. These are my observations from those two trips.

GROZNY, August 2000

Ruins rise under a hot sun. Piles of concrete line street after street. It's a strangely orderly scene of total destruction.

"I'm sick of hanging around here, playing cops and robbers.

I'm just trying to support my wife and buy an apartment," Sasha Tchesinov complains. Sasha is an officer in the Russian Ministry of the Interior, charged with maintaining order in Grozny. He will accompany me throughout my trip. A native of Volgograd, a town on the Volga River, Sasha is serving in Chechnya solely for the paycheck. He's thirty-five. His monthly salary is 3,500 rubles ($125), augmented by a 55 ruble-a-day ($2) bonus for duty in Chechnya. In addition, he is supposed to receive 1,000 rubles ($35) per day for his participation in Operation Antiterrorist. "But, as for the thousand rubles, there's been no sign of them since the beginning of the year," he grumbles. "In 1999, however, we did get our full pay."

I join Sasha and his men as they make their daily rounds in two armored vehicles. They always take the same route: a stop in the central market, a tour around the town, a trip past the station —one of the only reconstructed buildings in Grozny—and then back to the Russian base at Khankala, east of the city. Nothing would persuade these men to return to Grozny after dark. They know it's full of *boiviki*. "At night it's a crazy place, a giant fair where anything and everything can be bought, including human lives," Sasha says. I don't tell him that I know these ruins just about as well as he does. He is astonished that a young woman—a journalist, of course, but first and foremost, a woman—would think of coming to Chechnya. "The real war is finished. Now it's a war of mines. That's why it's calmer now," explains this young blond Rambo with his tinted glasses and shaved head. "We're all just waiting for it to be over."

According to local officials, several hundred people have come back to live in Grozny, but the place feels deserted. Here and there a decrepit kiosk has been knocked together. A few young women sell soda, bananas, and sunflower seeds in the street. Tattered apartment blocks line the principal boulevard, which has been rechristened "Gantamirov Prospekt" in honor of Bislan Gantamirov, a former mayor turned pro-Russian collaborator. There has been no electricity since February.

At the "Russian" city hall, no one wants to talk to the press. I can't get any concrete information on the exact number of inhabitants. Of course I do see people. The city center—the former site of the central bazaar—contains what little urban life there is. Women trudge along the side of the road, dragging metal containers of water on improvised carts. A few stalls offer the usual foodstuffs for sale. Tense-looking Russian soldiers dot the crowd, Kalachnikovs at the ready. Buses pick up and drop off passengers.

Kseta, a twenty-three-year-old woman with two babies in her arms, is having trouble stowing her belongings in the baggage compartment of a bus. No one offers to help her. "Things have certainly not got better since the spring," she says. "I would even say they're somewhat worse. Especially when it comes to the checkpoints all over the country. If their goal was to make our lives more difficult, they've certainly succeeded!" She hikes herself into the rusted bus that will deliver her back to the village of Toltsoy-Yurt, where her two older children are waiting for her. "This ticket costs 20 rubles! That's way too much!"

Khassam Isakov is squatting in the shade of his truck. He survived last winter's bombings by taking refuge with cousins north of the Terek River. He has returned to Grozny to spend the summer in the ruins of his house. "It's lucky that we've had no rain," he says with a smile, "because my roof couldn't possibly take it. And the Russians certainly don't help. They only make things harder for us," Khassam is talking loudly enough for Sasha to hear him. The latter, ill at ease, tries to pretend he's not listening. "At night," Khassam continues, "there are so many explosions we can't sleep." In his opinion, these are Russians firing at one another.

Next, Sasha takes me to the Minutka district, where I chat briefly with Ruslan Edisultanov, a policeman in the Gantamirov militia. Ruslan's not shy about speaking his mind: "Grozny is still the same hell hole. Nothing has changed! The bandits haven't left. I'd even say there are more of them now! Nobody seems to want the rule of law. What we need is a real leader, but we don't have one."

When we're back in the armored car, out of earshot, Sasha tries to pass Ruslan off as a madman: "He doesn't really believe what he's saying."

Before returning to the White House, the headquarters of the Interior Ministry's forces, Sasha makes a detour via checkpoint No. 8. Nine pale recruits are lined up before an instructor. They all look about fifteen years old. One of them, nineteen-year-old Yuri Vassilkov, explains timidly that he arrived here three months ago from a village in southern Russia. He suddenly breaks into crude but clear English. His superiors are at a loss for how to react; they're clearly proud that one of their recruits speaks a foreign language, but they're also embarrassed not to understand what he's saying. "It's getting more and more dangerous here," Yuri confides in English. "The counterattack could come at any moment.

Tonight, tomorrow, as we speak." I have a hard time stifling my urge to laugh.

The Russian army provides the foreign press with what they regard as their safest form of transportation: helicopter. In exchange, they maintain absolute control over our freedom of movement. My group of journalists has a long wait on the tarmac while the NCO's decide on our next destination. They finally opt for Borzoy, operational headquarters for the entire southern Caucasus region. It takes us less than forty-five minutes to fly from Khankala to Borzoy, high in the mountains near the Georgian border. There we get a relaxed, even chummy welcome, which, as usual, rings false. "Look around you," exclaims Colonel Andrei Fiodorov, indicating the mountains encircling our high plateau. "Here we are in Switzerland. Chechnya is our little Switzerland!"

Fiodorov invites us into his tent, where the heat is almost unbearable. He is red in the face and sweating heavily. I note the five telephones on a small stand next to his desk. "We've been here since May," he says, wiping his forehead. "Our military presence here is completely normal. After all, it's our home territory. Just another part of Russia." When several journalists point out, by way of objection, that other parts of Russia have no antiterrorist operation, he simply repeats himself lamely: "Our status here is no different from anywhere else in Russia. Moreover, there's nothing going on. It's been calm here for more than a month and a half, when our last soldier was killed."

The Federals stationed permanently in Chechnya make up the Russian 42nd Division. The division is 15,000 men strong. According to Fiodorov, it is better trained and equipped than other Russian fighting units. He will not, however, supply details: "Our equipment was good enough to get us to this point," he says blandly. The men under his command at Borzoy, whose exact numbers remain secret, are divided equally between raw recruits with no prior experience and *kontraktniki* ("contract soldiers"), who fought in the previous Russo-Chechen war.

The soldiers I run into admit that they hear automatic gunfire every night from the rebels hiding in the surrounding areas. But according to Fiodorov, the Russians have already won the war. "As far as we're concerned, the real victory was the recent election," he says.* "People voted, which is to say that they're with us, the Russians." He's wrong. In reality, the Chechens express total indifference to the election, or else they call it "a farce." Fiodorov chooses to ignore that fact. Instead, he remains optimistic that the coming winter will be "easy." "The bandits are putting up no resistance. Summer was the big hurdle, and it's behind us. Now that the leaves are off the trees, they won't be able to pass through here [to Georgia], and they'll need to worry about food, so they'll be even more visible."

Despite his attempts to be upbeat, Fiodorov admits that the Russian military is preparing for a long-term presence in Chechnya. "We're in the process of building permanent installations not far from this camp. They'll be ready in the autumn. We're employing the local population in their construction. There will be housing for families and schools. I'm going to be able to send for my wife and daughter!" He smiles at the thought.

---

* The August 20, 2000, election for a local deputy to the Moscow Duma.

As we prepare to set off again in the helicopter, I hear him mutter: "In any case, I'm only here for two years, maximum. That's a piece of luck!"

We fly back to Khankala, spend the night, and leave by car the next morning for Tsentora-Yurt, about thirty kilometers south of Gudermes. We are to meet with Akhmed Kadyrov, who has been appointed to head Moscow's administration in Chechnya. It's a fine afternoon and we wait for Kadyrov out on the veranda of a brick house set in the hills not far from the border with Dagestan. Inside, twenty-five men sit cross-legged on carpets covering the concrete floor. They wear *piess* (prayer caps) and sway from side to side. Their eyes are half closed. Their lips move as they chant prayers for their country, prayers for an end to war. Kadyrov sits among them, grave and silent, surrounded by his father and older cousins. He has invited these members of his *teip* (family clan) and some political associates to his home for his birthday. Now the oldest man present, Kadyrov's bearded father, raises his palms to heaven in a final prayer to the glory of Allah.

As the ceremony finishes, women come forward to unroll oil-cloths over the rugs. They bring out dishes of lamb, burning-hot potatoes, and garlic sauce. Akhmed Kadyrov is dressed in gray. His feet are bare. He has a crafty look, and though he's in the bosom of his family, he doesn't hesitate to talk tough. "At present my administration has no control to speak of," he says. "But I have an agent in every village, something that Maskhadov can't boast of." He pauses, then points at the men around him, who are hanging on his every word. "Any one of them could be a Maskhadov agent," he says, raising his voice. "I can't really be sure who all these men are working for. It isn't written on their faces. Enemy agents are everywhere and nowhere at the same time!"

Akhmed Kadyrov knows what he's talking about. He has already survived several assassination attempts. The last one occurred in June, when a man carrying a bomb was intercepted only a few meters from his house. The "traitor" was arrested and thrown into prison. "It was a Maskhadov man. They had promised him $6,000 for my life," Kadyrov asserts grimly. He harbors obvious bitterness toward the Chechen president.

"Working together, we Chechens must stop this conflict," Kadyrov continues. "If we don't, the fighting will go on for at least another ten years. We must halt the arms-bearers and try to reintegrate them into normal life. But we can't kid ourselves: Chechen citizens are hiding and feeding these criminals. If citizens would close their doors, the fighters would end up on the streets with no place to hide. That's the only way we can make progress."

It's unlikely that Kadyrov's opinions will be heeded. The pro-Russian bureaucrat is not very popular in his own country, and his administration doesn't even have a police force. During the first Russo-Chechen conflict, Kadyrov supported the pro-independence rebels and he threw his weight behind Aslan Maskhadov in the presidential elections of 1997; but last fall Kadyrov changed sides. He explains his change of heart unapologetically: "In this war, I'm on the side of the people. I should point out that in the preceding war I was also on the side of the people. It's the people who have changed their minds, not I. In 1994, the people were in the streets. In their demonstrations and gatherings, they were supporting the *boiviki*. Today the situation has completely changed.

We're the ones who violated the cease-fire accord signed by Maskhadov and Yeltsin when we attacked Dagestan. Aslan [Maskhadov] should have prevented Shamil [Bassayev] from going into Dagestan. He was the president, after all. But he didn't even condemn that invasion! In short, I withdrew my support from the rebels when I realized that Maskhadov himself wanted war."

As a result of his changing sides, Kadyrov has very little support from either camp. The rebels feel he betrayed them, and the Russians still think of him as a "bandit." The civilian population simply ignores him.

In a few days, Kadyrov is planning to leave for the United States to participate in an Islamic conference. "I want to meet the leaders of the Arab world who think that what we have here is a religious war," he tells me vehemently. "I've got to make them understand that what's happening here is not at all what they think. They must stop financing the bandits!"

A man interrupts to whisper a few words in Kadyrov's ear. Kadyrov excuses himself, explaining that he must leave immediately. His black Nissan Patrol with its tinted windows is already waiting outside. Vladimir Putin, the Russian president, wants him on the telephone.

INGUSHETIA, September 2000

I'm travelling alone, as I did during my earlier visits, before I was deported by the FSB. This time I don't even have Islam with me. He's not doing well. He seems more confused and depressed than ever. He's convinced that there is no future for him in Chechnya and he's tired of the fighting. He wants to go away, somewhere, anywhere. He wants to put this war behind him, to get some kind of professional training, to acquire some skill. He wants to feel calm and safe. Then he'll come back and watch his son grow up.

Islam doesn't want me to cross over into Chechnya without him. He's worried and also a little jealous. I promise him that I'll look up some of our mutual friends, and that I'll come back safe and sound.

STARYE ATAGI, *September 2000*

"It's not a war; it's a collective assassination. They're killing us little by little." Andarbek Bakayev, chief of surgery at the Starye Atagi hospital, doesn't mince words. A thirty-eight year-old with dark circles under his eyes, Andarbek seems to have lost all hope of an early end to the Russo-Chechen conflict. He chain-smokes as he tells his story in a hollow voice: "On September 7, a group of fifteen masked Russians broke into the hospital around seven in the morning. They pointed to one of my patients, who had been here since last March, Edilbek Issayev. He was a young man—thirty-three years old—who had been wounded by shell fragments and was still on crutches. They promised me they'd bring him back. Six days later, a local farmer came across a common grave in one of his fields. Edilbek's body was on top of three other corpses—all young men who had recently disappeared." Andarbek stares ahead blankly. He doesn't want to know whether his patient was a *boivik* or not. But he's sure of one thing: This war isn't like other wars. "There's no front, no enemy you can see."

Since the rebel fighters poured out of Grozny in early February, leaving the city to the Russians, skirmishes between the Federals and groups of armed rebels have ceased. Now the Russians are terrorizing the civilian population. In every Chechen village, young men have disappeared in the course of the *zatchiska* ("cleansing operations"). The lucky ones return, several thousand dollars lighter, with only bruises; the unlucky ones don't come back at all.

Last May, two former officials of the Chechen parliament were detained and abused at the Khankala base near Grozny, the headquarters of the Russian forces. One of them tells me their story: "They arrested us, without any official reason, at a checkpoint and took us to Urus-Martan. There, at the *kommandantura*, they exhibited us to some Russian television reporters. They said that we were *boiviki*. Then they transferred us by helicopter to Khankala, where they took us to a trailer. It had the word "café" written on it, but in fact it was our prison for ten days. They kept us in handcuffs and made us stand up straight with our backs against a wall. We couldn't sit at all. They wouldn't even let us go to the toilet; our jailers gave us a bottle to use when we needed it. We had nothing to eat or drink, except, maybe five or six times, a tin of something or a little water. There were six other prisoners, younger than we were. At night men from the Moscow OMON (special forces of the Interior Ministry) in black hoods would beat them. My friend and I were lucky, maybe because we were older, they didn't beat us. I still don't know if the others survived."

One of the two officials had $1,800 on him at the time of his "arrest." He had to turn the money over to an officer before they would let him go. The Russians then demanded $5,000 and three machine guns for the "liberation" of his colleague.

Heading for the southern mountains, I pass through some fifteen control posts. I'm on my way to a rebel-held village in search of Aslan Maskhadov. Though surrounded on all sides by Russian troops, the village is buried so deep in the forest that it has remained under *boivik* control. Since they left Grozny, the Chechen fighters have lain low. They have yet to mount a counteroffensive. They remain grouped in mobile rapid-attack units in and around such villages. The Russians are aware of their presence but neither side attacks.

I head south, hoping I won't have too much trouble finding Maskhadov. This kind of travel demands patience. As I near the village, five male forms emerge out of the thick fog. One of them is using a chainsaw to cut tree trunks along the roadside as two others observe his progress. Maulli is twenty-five. Like his comrades, he fought with the *boiviki* in the earlier war. This time he refuses to join them. "They don't even know what they're doing. They're not fighting for an idea as they did the last time," Maulli explains. "In the first place, I don't like the way this war started." He runs his eyes around the circle of men around him. "All of us here would willingly fight the Russians for our independence," he states firmly, "but not as long as Shamil [Bassayev] is leading the troops."

Maulli's companion, Khussein, agrees. He worked between the two wars as a driver in Khattab's training camp at Serjen-Yurt. "Back then I made pretty good money, $100 a week. But it all ended last fall, when I refused to join up again with the rebel fighters," he explains.

While the young men from the mountains refuse to go back to war, they do offer indirect help to the rebels. Zulikhan, the wife of one of them, has "relations with the *boiviki*," as she puts it. Every other day she takes the bus down the plain to the market at Gudermes. There she fills orders for the rebel fighters. They need the basics, such as flour, but also jogging suits, caps, and audiotapes. "I mark up the goods by a third and sell them back to the rebels. This business allows me to feed my family," she explains. "They pay cash. Logistics are the only problem. I can't, for example, carry six pairs of trousers at a time. That would attract attention at the checkpoints. So I have to transport the goods little by little." Recently, Zulikhan crossed paths with the Arab rebel leader Khattab, who looks "much thinner but still in good shape." She also met Shamil Bassayev and his brother Sharvani in a large insurgent group.

Most Chechens seem uncertain about how things will turn out. "It's deceptively calm, as if nothing were happening," says one of the village men. "In fact, there's a lot going on that we don't know about. I wouldn't be surprised to learn of clandestine negotiations between the Russians and the rebels. Both groups are here, and they each do exactly as they please. We're the ones who have to pay the piper."

I finally find Maskhadov. He is wearing a military uniform with a pistol in his belt and appears to be in perfect health. Seated on a comfortable sofa in a "safe house," he seems relaxed and eager to share his thoughts on the situation in Chechnya. Outside, Russian armored vehicles pass through the autumn mist. Since he left Grozny the previous winter, the rebel president hasn't spent more than two consecutive days in any one spot. He usually communicates with his men and with the outside world by means of audiotapes. Few journalists take the trouble to hunt him down and interview him. In any case, he's very suspicious of the press. We talk for several hours over a meal of soup.

"The Russian intervention in Chechnya is about one year old. Where are we now?" I ask Maskhadov.

The fugitive leader answers simply: "As far as we're concerned, it all began on September 5, 1999, when the Russians bombed our country for the first time, and not on October 1. This time we're not so naïve as to throw ourselves into all-out combat with the Russians, as we did in the first war. We know that's not the way to make any headway against their army. All we can do is mount a series diversionary actions," he explains. "Our goal is not to halt their army but to conserve our own forces. While they occupy our territory—that is, while they remain inactive—their forces grow weaker, while ours get stronger. Our men are everywhere. The Russians know it, and yet they never mount an offensive. Their army is demoralized."

I ask Maskhadov why the rebels didn't counterattack during the summer when it would have been easier. "We intended to. We had set plans for retaking Grozny and Gudermes and Argun," he answers. "But at a meeting of the GKO,* we opted for guerilla action instead. Our strength lies in our invisibility, when we're everywhere and nowhere at the same time. We also want to keep

---

* The State Defense Committee, comprising some forty key leaders of secessionist Chechnya.

our losses to a minimum. It's not in Russia's interest to continue this war, but she can't stop now without admitting defeat. Putin must have understood by now that the generals who promised him a quick victory are good-for-nothings, but he can't officially acknowledge that fact. It would be too great an embarrassment."

Maskhadov is so involved in his thoughts that he has forgotten all about his soup. It has grown cold. He pushes his bowl aside and leans forward. He wants to talk about the retreat from Grozny in early February. "I never ever said that they should defend the city to the last man," he tells me. "Our reason for staying in Grozny was political, not strategic. We demonstrated our bravery to the world in defending the capital, but there are limits to bravery. I had a completely different plan in mind for our withdrawal, and it's true that I didn't anticipate so many losses. However, since we left Grozny, the situation has become stagnant. The Russians are trying tactics from the earlier war, but without success. Their first stage was the military campaign. It failed because the 'bandits' and the 'terrorists' are still at large. In the second stage, the Russians introduced the political puppets who they hoped would provoke discord among us, Kadyrov and Gantamirov. Now we're at the third stage: We're holding elections to the Duma. The next stage will be negotiations, no doubt about it. To think that I warned Yeltsin that he would be better advised to make friends with the Chechens!"

Maskhadov is silent for a moment. He lets out a deep sigh. The Chechens, he admits, are tired of this war. "I recognize that the situation is difficult for the civilian population, which has become the target of the Russian army. I also regret that thousands of my countrymen have had to leave for Ingushetia or elsewhere. But each time I send out my representatives, they come back with the same message: 'Continue the fight. We're with you.' We can't afford to lose face, and the population knows it as well as I do. One way or another, the Russians will be forced to come to the negotiating table. I am constantly reminding Putin that he'll be better off negotiating with me, as long as I'm alive. It will be worse without me. And the Russians will leave in the end. Last time they led us to believe that they would never leave and then they disappeared. The worse thing would be if they stayed and we had to defend their troops here in Chechnya!"

After a moment's thought, he continues: "This time I will make it a point of honor that any accord we sign includes international guarantees. Putin behaves very strangely, you know. He misled his own people in the Kursk affair.* I know the generals who are waging this second campaign. They were already here in '94. In their place, I would die of shame. For a start, they avoid all contact with the enemy, with us. And then they're making money off the war. It's the only thing they're interested in. They take out their aggression on innocent civilians. As soon as the military learns that *boiviki* are in a certain area, they cease firing. They're scared to death. That's why I always say to the village chiefs, 'Whatever you do, don't admit that you're not harboring rebel fighters. They'll bombard you. Tell them instead that you're hiding at least two hundred rebels. That way they'll leave you alone.'" With that, Maskhadov breaks out in laughter.

---

* A Russian nuclear submarine that sank in August 2000, trapping all 118 crew members on board. Putin was criticized for several failed rescue attempts and his own slow reaction to the disaster.

"In the past, I formally forbade our troops to open fire from the village centers. The Russians soon figured out what was going on and took advantage of the situation. So not long ago I reversed the order. Better that we ourselves should open fire than that we should stand by silently while the Russians rob and pillage and commit acts of barbarism. We have exactly 420 villages in Chechnya. In each one of them we have at least fifty combatants and thirty or so reservists. That's around 33,000 persons I can count on, in addition to my commanders and their staffs. I coordinate all operations and try to maintain discipline. That's the most important thing. At the Russian headquarters, the generals spread out their military maps at night, but in the field the next day, the adjutants don't follow their orders. That's the problem with the Russian army: The soldiers don't want to die!" Maskhadov assures me.

Maskhadov repudiates the idea of a religious component to the conflict. "This is a war of national liberation. We are fighting to deprive Russia of the right to destroy us as a nation. I'm forty-nine years old. I've lived through the Chechen deportation and two wars. I know what I'm talking about. We're followers of Islam, but 'Wahhabism' isn't part of our tradition. Chechens are not going to let themselves be turned into Arabs."

Maskhadov is enjoying our discussion. It's rare that he has the full attention of a member of the foreign press. He has a hard time tearing himself away, but he finally gets up to leave, followed by his Minister of Defense and two bodyguards. His old car starts up crankily. It carries him away to the edge of the forest. From there he will go on horseback to his camp.

MOSCOW, January 2001

In my coverage of this war, I have tried to avoid assigning guilt to one side or the other. Instead, I have tried to show that the Russo-Chechen conflict will not cease until first the Russians and then the rest of the international community work toward that end.

Though the Russians have lacked dramatic military success in this latest conflict, they have won the propaganda war. They have managed to confuse the West by representing their "Operation Antiterrorist" as an effort to save the southern reaches of Russia from Islamic terrorism. Is this fair to the Chechens? Who are the Chechen enemy? Bloodthirsty rebels who would impose the *charia* on their neighbors at any cost? Or confused and isolated men and women, who dream of only one thing: an end to this conflict so that their children can return to school and "normal" life can resume?

A minority of secessionist Chechens will indeed fight to the bitter end. They will continue to prey upon the Russian troops as long as the Russians are present in Chechnya. But the majority of the Chechen population longs to put an end to the killing. We must look to them to convince the Russians to find a solution to this conflict. We must not forget the countless humiliations and acts of violence that these Chechens suffer in their daily lives.

Index

PublicAffairs is a new nonfiction publishing house and a tribute to the standards, values, and flair of three persons who have served as mentors to countless reporters, writers, editors, and book people of all kinds, including me.

I.F. STONE, proprietor of *I. F. Stone's Weekly*, combined a commitment to the First Amendment with entrepreneurial zeal and reporting skill and became one of the great independent journalists in American history. At the age of eighty, Izzy published *The Trial of Socrates,* which was a national bestseller. He wrote the book after he taught himself ancient Greek.

BENJAMIN C. BRADLEE was for nearly thirty years the charismatic editorial leader of *The Washington Post.* It was Ben who gave the *Post* the range and courage to pursue such historic issues as Watergate. He supported his reporters with a tenacity that made them fearless and it is no accident that so many became authors of influential, best-selling books.

ROBERT L. BERNSTEIN, the chief executive of Random House for more than a quarter century, guided one of the nation's premier publishing houses. Bob was personally responsible for many books of political dissent and argument that challenged tyranny around the globe. He is also the founder and longtime chair of Human Rights Watch, one of the most respected human rights organizations in the world.

≙

For fifty years, the banner of Public Affairs Press was carried by its owner Morris B. Schnapper, who published Gandhi, Nasser, Toynbee, Truman and about 1,500 other authors. In 1983, Schnapper was described by *The Washington Post* as "a redoubtable gadfly." His legacy will endure in the books to come.

Peter Osnos, *Publisher*

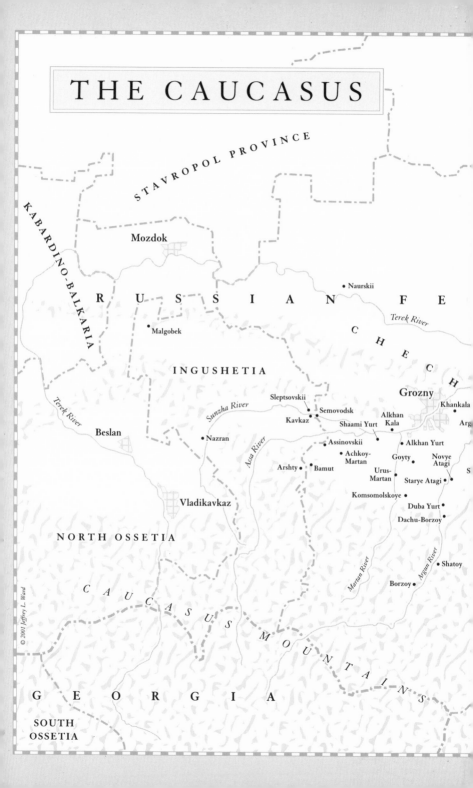

THE CAUCASUS

STAVROPOL PROVINCE

KABARDINO-BALKARIA

Mozdok

• Naurskii

R U S S I A N   F E

Terek River

CHECH

• Malgobek

INGUSHETIA

Grozny

Khankala

Sleptsovskii

Sunzha River

Kavkaz • • Semovodsk

Shaami Yurt

Alkhan Kala

Arg

Terek River

Beslan

• Nazran

Assa River

• Assinovskii

• Alkhan Yurt

Arshty • • Bamut

• Achkoy-Martan

Goyty •

Novye Atagi •

Urus-Martan

S

• Starye Atagi

Vladikavkaz

• Komsomolskoye

Duba Yurt •

Dachu-Borzoy •

NORTH OSSETIA

C A U C A S U S

Martan River

Argun River

• Shatoy

Borzoy •

M O U N T A I N S

G E O R G I A

SOUTH OSSETIA

© 2001 Jeffrey L. Ward